The Six Sigma Manual

for Small and Medium Businesses

What You Need to Know Explained Simply

By Craig Baird

THE SIX SIGMA MANUAL FOR SMALL AND MEDIUM BUSINESSES:
WHAT YOU NEED TO KNOW EXPLAINED SIMPLY

Copyright © 2009 by Atlantic Publishing Group, Inc.
1405 SW 6th Ave. • Ocala, Florida 34471 • 800-814-1132 • 352-622-1875–Fax
Web site: www.atlantic-pub.com • E-mail: sales@atlantic-pub.com
SAN Number: 268-1250

No part of this publication may be reproduced, stored in a retrieval system, or transmitted in any form or by any means, electronic, mechanical, photocopying, recording, scanning, or otherwise, except as permitted under Section 107 or 108 of the 1976 United States Copyright Act, without the prior written permission of the Publisher. Requests to the Publisher for permission should be sent to Atlantic Publishing Group, Inc., 1405 SW 6th Ave., Ocala, Florida 34471.

ISBN-13: 978-1-60138-233-7   ISBN-10: 1-60138-233-2

Library of Congress Cataloging-in-Publication Data

Baird, Craig W., 1980-
 The six sigma manual for small and medium businesses : what you need
to know explained simply / Craig W. Baird.
    p. cm.
 Includes bibliographical references and index.
 ISBN-13: 978-1-60138-233-7 (alk. paper)
 ISBN-10: 1-60138-233-2 (alk. paper)
 1. Small business--Management. 2. Six sigma (Quality control
standard) 3. Total quality management. I. Title.
 HD62.7.B327 2009
 658.4'013--dc22
                                                            2008038307

LIMIT OF LIABILITY/DISCLAIMER OF WARRANTY: The publisher and the author make no representations or warranties with respect to the accuracy or completeness of the contents of this work and specifically disclaim all warranties, including without limitation warranties of fitness for a particular purpose. No warranty may be created or extended by sales or promotional materials. The advice and strategies contained herein may not be suitable for every situation. This work is sold with the understanding that the publisher is not engaged in rendering legal, accounting, or other professional services. If professional assistance is required, the services of a competent professional should be sought. Neither the publisher nor the author shall be liable for damages arising herefrom. The fact that an organization or Web site is referred to in this work as a citation and/or a potential source of further information does not mean that the author or the publisher endorses the information the organization or Web site may provide or recommendations it may make. Further, readers should be aware that Internet Web sites listed in this work may have changed or disappeared between when this work was written and when it is read.

BOOK MANAGER: Melissa Peterson • mpeterson@atlantic-pub.com
INTERIOR LAYOUT DESIGN: Nicole Deck • ndeck@atlantic-pub.com

Printed in the United States

We recently lost our beloved pet "Bear," who was not only our best and dearest friend but also the "Vice President of Sunshine" here at Atlantic Publishing. He did not receive a salary but worked tirelessly 24 hours a day to please his parents. Bear was a rescue dog that turned around and showered myself, my wife Sherri, his grandparents Jean, Bob and Nancy and every person and animal he met (maybe not rabbits) with friendship and love. He made a lot of people smile every day.

We wanted you to know that a portion of the profits of this book will be donated to The Humane Society of the United States. *—Douglas & Sherri Brown*

The human-animal bond is as old as human history. We cherish our animal companions for their unconditional affection and acceptance. We feel a thrill when we glimpse wild creatures in their natural habitat or in our own backyard.

Unfortunately, the human-animal bond has at times been weakened. Humans have exploited some animal species to the point of extinction.

The Humane Society of the United States makes a difference in the lives of animals here at home and worldwide. The HSUS is dedicated to creating a world where our relationship with animals is guided by compassion. We seek a truly humane society in which animals are respected for their intrinsic value, and where the human-animal bond is strong.

Want to help animals? We have plenty of suggestions. Adopt a pet from a local shelter, join The Humane Society and be a part of our work to help companion animals and wildlife. You will be funding our educational, legislative, investigative and outreach projects in the U.S. and across the globe.

Or perhaps you'd like to make a memorial donation in honor of a pet, friend or relative? You can through our Kindred Spirits program. And if you'd like to contribute in a more structured way, our Planned Giving Office has suggestions about estate planning, annuities, and even gifts of stock that avoid capital gains taxes.

Maybe you have land that you would like to preserve as a lasting habitat for wildlife. Our Wildlife Land Trust can help you. Perhaps the land you want to share is a backyard—that's enough. Our Urban Wildlife Sanctuary Program will show you how to create a habitat for your wild neighbors.

So you see, it's easy to help animals. And The HSUS is here to help.

THE HUMANE SOCIETY OF THE UNITED STATES

2100 L Street NW • Washington, DC 20037 • 202-452-1100
www.hsus.org

Table of Contents

Introduction — 13

What is Six Sigma? 13

Six Sigma As Opposed to Total Quality Management 20

Why Your Business Needs Six Sigma 22

How This Book Is Organized 26

Section 1: Six Sigma Overview — 29

Section Introduction 30

Chapter 1: The Innovation of Six Sigma — 33

Process Improvement 38

Customer Focus 39

Chapter 2: The Language of Six Sigma — 45

Critical to X 47

Critical to Quality 50

Design of Experiments 52

Internal Rate of Return 56

Metrics 58

Voice of the Customer 58

Defects per Million Opportunities 59

SIPOC 59

Chapter 3: The Formula for Success   63

Chapter Introduction 63

Using the Scientific Method to Understand Six Sigma 64

Scientific Method as a Model
for Understanding Six Sigma 66

Chapter 4: Six Sigma Modeling   69

The Six Phases of Six Sigma 70

Section Conclusion 81

Section 2: Six Sigma Leadership   83

Chapter 5: Are You Ready for Six Sigma?   85

Attitudes and Organization
Structures Necessary for Six Sigma 86

Chapter 6: Managers and Six Sigma   91

Support from the Top 92

How Six Sigma Benefits Managers 94

Champions 94

Implementation Leaders 96

Chapter 7: The Six Sigma Team — 99

Master Black Belts 101

Black Belts 103

Training a Black Belt 106

Green Belts 108

Yellow Belts 110

Chapter 8: Team Training — 113

Leadership Training.. 116

Black Belt Training 117

Green Belt Training 118

Skills Needed by Both Belts 118

Evaluation 119

Reinforcement 120

Refreshers 121

Section Conclusion 123

Section 3: Understanding DMAIC — 127

Section Introduction 128

Chapter 9: Define — 131

The Basics 132

The Problem 133

Who Defines Projects? 134

The Mistakes and the Steps 134

Understand the Magnitude 137

Weigh the Costs 139

The Problem Statement 140

Project Objective 142

Launching the Project 144

Chapter 10: Measure — 147

Understanding Statistics 148

Mode 149

Mean or Average 150

Median 150

Range 151

Process Metrics 153

Critical to Quality 154

Critical to Cost 154

Critical to Schedule 156

Chapter 11: Analyze — 159

Value Stream Analysis 162

Process Complexities 163

Reducing Non-Value Activities 166

Analyzing Sources of Variations 170

ANOVA and Nested ANOVA 175

Chapter 12: Improve — 177

Defining New Operating Procedures 178

Running Simulations 179

Finding the Benefits of the Solution 182

Chapter 13: Control — 185

Monitoring Processes 187

Operational Procedures 188

Training 190

The Importance of Control Plans 191

Section Conclusion 193

Section 4: Understanding DMADV — 195

Section Introduction 196

Chapter 14: Define and Measure — 201

Chapter 15: Analyze — 207

The Tasks 208

Using Customer Demands to Design 209

Chapter 16: Design and Verify — 213

Simulating the Processes 215

Verifying Everything 217

Section Conclusion 219

Section 5: Lean Six Sigma — 221

Section Introduction 222

Chapter 17: The Principles of Lean — 225

Defects 226

Overproduction 226

Inventories 227

Unnecessary Processing 228

Unnecessary Movement of People 228

Unnecessary Transport of Goods 229

Waiting 229

The Laws of Lean Six Sigma 230

Chapter 18: Becoming a Lean Business — 233

The Lean Lessons 234

Lean Tips 239

Chapter 19: Kaizen Methodology — 241

Section Conclusion 245

Section 6: Other Six Sigma Models — 247

Section Introduction 248

MAIC 249

DCCDI 249

DCDOV 250

IDOV 250

DMADOV 251

CDOV 252

Section Conclusion 253

Six Sigma Glossary — 257

Bibliography — 281

Dedication & Author Biography — 283

Index — 285

Foreword

With The Six Sigma Manual for Small and Medium Businesses, Craig Baird makes the often mysterious and complex concepts and approaches of Six Sigma accessible for people engaged in making smaller companies grow and prosper.

While Six Sigma has been around for over 20 years, it has largely been embraced by larger companies. Craig makes a solid case for how small and medium businesses can and should benefit and then breaks the Six Sigma essentials into smaller topics that can be easily understood. He provides guidance on how to apply these approaches to situations that are relevant for these companies.

Introducing the terminology for Six Sigma in a straightforward way and delving into the steps involved in the DMAIC improvement process and the Lean methods with a breezy, relaxed style, this book can help anyone working for a small or medium sized business understand how Six Sigma and the DMAIC steps can help improve their financial results and satisfy, or even delight, their customers.

Recognizing the broad range products and services provided by small and medium businesses, The Six Sigma Manual for Small and Medium Businesses also provides an overview of Design for

Six Sigma (DFSS) and Lean methods that might be very useful to some businesses.

Small and medium businesses generate the most jobs and the most growth all over the world; the opportunity to help these businesses move to a higher level of achievement, a higher level of profitability and growth, and a higher level of customer engagement through the proven Six Sigma processes …this is a worthy goal.

Eric C. Maass, PhD

Director and Lead Master Black Belt, DFSS

Motorola, Inc.

Introduction

"Effective leadership is putting first things first. Effective management is discipline, carrying it out."

-Stephen Covey

What is Six Sigma?

When you go up to someone and ask him or her what Six Sigma is, this person will most likely give you a strange look, may state it is a fraternity, or may simply tell you he or she has no idea what it is.

Despite the fact that it is a revolutionary concept, Six Sigma is little understood or known by the common public.

You should not let this lack of renown bother you, because like the best secrets, those individuals who need to know about Six Sigma will know about it, and the fact you are reading this book shows that you want to know what Six Sigma can offer to you.

In the plainest terms, Six Sigma is a set of practices developed by Motorola to improve processes by eliminating defects. What is a defect? A defect is defined as anything that is nonconforming on a product or service relative to the specifications of the product or service.

The history of Six Sigma will be addressed later. Right now, the focus is on defining it.

Normally, Six Sigma will assert the following:

- Continuous efforts to reduce variation in process outputs are the key to business success.

- Manufacturing and business processes can be measured, analyzed, improved, and controlled.

- Succeeding at achieving sustained quality improvement requires commitment from everyone in the organization, including top-level management.

What do those mean? They are a bit more complicated than they need to be for an explanation, so here they are in simplified form:

- Improving customer satisfaction

- Reducing cycle time

- Reducing defects

This, then, begs the question, why is it called Six Sigma? What is Six Sigma? All of these will be addressed early in the book, but to answer the first question, Six Sigma refers to the ability of highly capable processes to output within specification. This means that processes operating with Six Sigma quality produce at defect levels of below 3.4 defects per one million opportunities. Six Sigma's goal is to improve some key processes to that level of quality or better.

Introduction

If you can have a process that is below 3.4 defects per one million opportunities or products, you are incredibly efficient; this amounts to 0.00034 percent. To show just how incredibly efficient the Six Sigma strategy is, look at a few other odds:

ODDS	
Odds of defect in Six Sigma process product:	34,000 to 1
Odds of bowling a 300 game:	11,500 to 1
Odds of getting a hole-in-one:	5,000 to 1
Odds of injury during fireworks:	19,556 to 1
Odds of injury during shaving:	6,585 to 1
Odds of injury from a chainsaw:	4,464 to 1
Odds of being murdered:	18,000 to 1
Odds of being on a plane with a drunk pilot:	117 to 1
Odds of winning an Academy Award:	11,500 to 1
*Odds from **http://www.funny2.com/odds.htm**	

These odds are not to show you how unlikely it is that you can get Six Sigma working for you; that is not the point. The point is that you can use Six Sigma to get these odds, and because of how incredibly efficient the Six Sigma odds are, there is no chance about it. It is all about learning how Six Sigma works and applying it to your own business so you can achieve the same results.

Going back to the three points outlined earlier in the book, what do they represent to your business? When a business has higher customer satisfaction, it has more customers and better word of mouth spreading about it.

When a business has lower turnover, that business has more productivity. When a business has a low amount of defects, the company is incredibly efficient.

When all of these come together for a company, it allows that company to achieve dramatic cost savings, while presenting itself with opportunities to retain customers, capture new markets, and build a reputation as one of the top companies in its sector, whether the company sells a service or product.

It can be easy to look at this and think that Six Sigma is about quality control, but truly it is not. Six Sigma is not a quality initiative; it is a business initiative and it has the expressed goal of achieving many small and incremental improvements while pushing for breakthroughs in other areas of the business operations. This is why when a company is said to "reach Six Sigma," it is performing with nearly no defects. Remember the stat? The 3.4-per-one-million statistic is a low number.

Looking at Six Sigma and what has been written here, has the question of Six Sigma been answered? It is a way to improve the efficiency and productivity of a business, but you need to go a bit further, and that involves delving into the wonderful world of statistics.

Six Sigma is a method, but also a statistical measure - and the concept of standard deviation has a big part to play.

Standard deviation is the way to describe any variation in a set group of data. When you weigh bags of potatoes of different sizes, you will have a higher standard deviation than if you weigh bags of potatoes of all the same size. Why? There is a greater difference between the weight of the bags (5-, 10-, and 20-pound bags) if they are different than if they are the same (three 5-pound bags). Another way to look at this is through a parcel delivery company. When you tell a customer that you will have the parcel delivered between Tuesday and Wednesday, you are allowing the customer to prepare himself or herself to be home on those two days. You agree through the contract that if you deliver the parcel on Monday or Thursday, the customer will receive a 50 percent discount, while you provide a bonus to delivery truck drivers who get the parcel there on those two days.

Six Sigma works the same way. If you deliver your parcels on time only 69 percent of the time, you sit at a low Sigma level, around Two Sigma (do not worry, the levels will be addressed later). Now, if you deliver your products on time about 94 percent of the time, you are still only at a Three Sigma level. Now, if you can deliver the products on time 99.4 percent of the time, you are up to a Four Sigma level. This is an incredibly high efficiency rate, but it is not high enough to be considered Six Sigma.

If you can deliver your parcels on time, 99.9997 percent of the time, you will have reached Six Sigma level. That is an incredibly high level of efficiency, which means that for every one million parcels delivered, only three to four arrive late. This means that not only do you have high customer satisfaction, but you will also be able to have discount rates to customers for the parcels arriving late or too early.

On top of that, you will have extremely happy employees because they will be getting bonuses on those on-time deliveries. Do not worry, as the high customer satisfaction and referral rates will more than offset the costs of the bonuses to your employees.

This shows that Six Sigma was developed to assist in:

- Focusing on the paying customers of a business. Oddly, companies do not always follow this procedure, and traditionally, labor hours, costs, and sales volume have been more important in the evaluation of things that the customer does not truly care about.

- Providing a way to measure and compare different processes within the company. This will allow you, in the terms of the delivery company, to look at the delivery and processing parts of the entire operation. They are different in what they do, but both parts are incredibly important to making the company successful.

More detail about Sigma levels will be addressed later on, but this introduction will provide you with a quick and easy guide while you assess what level your business is currently sitting at in terms of Sigma.

SIGMA LEVEL	DEFECTS PER MILLION	EFFICIENCY PERCENTAGE
Six	3.4	99.99966 percent
Five	233	99.9767 percent
Four	6,210	99.379 percent
Three	66,807	93.3193 percent
Two	308,537	69.1463 percent
One	690,000	31 percent

As you can see from the chart, Six, Five, and Four Sigma is efficient. Most companies would love to have anything over 99 percent efficiency, but being a part of the Six Sigma world is all about achieving the top level of efficiency possible. Even Three Sigma is above 93 percent efficiency, and that is also excellent.

However, Two and One Sigma take a noticeable drop, and any company that operates with an efficiency below 70 percent is in serious trouble with low customer satisfaction, high defects, and poor productivity.

Introduction

Below is a graph showing how well-known activities and industries fair on the Six Sigma level, luckily, flight fatality has the highest Sigma Level. At a 6.7 sigma level, you can fly every day for 21,000 years without an accident.

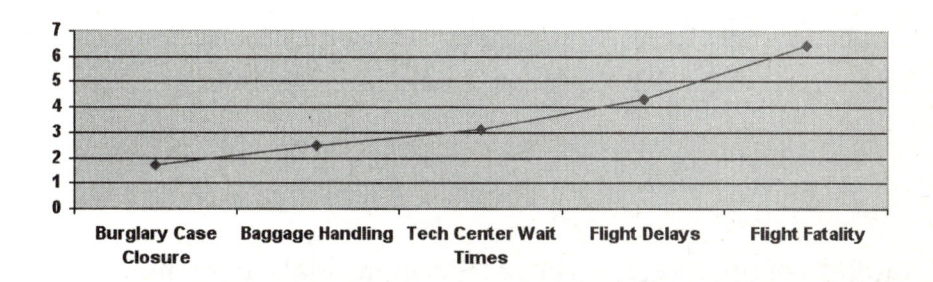

[Graph showing Sigma levels for: Burglary Case Closure (~1.8), Baggage Handling (~2.5), Tech Center Wait Times (~3.1), Flight Delays (~4.2), Flight Fatality (~6.4)]

COMPANIES THAT USE SIX SIGMA	
Company	Most Recent Revenue Figures
3M	$22.6 billion
Amazon.com	$14.84 billion
Bank of America	$119.19 billion
Boeing	$61.5 billion
Caterpillar	$44.958 billion
Dell	$57.095 billion
DuPont	$28.98 billion
Ford Motor Company	$173.9 billion
General Electric	$172.738 billion
LG Group	$94.8 billion
Merrill Lynch	$70.59 billion
Motorola	$43.739 billion
Samsung Group	$153.2 billion
Siemens AG	$110.82 billion
United States Air Force	N/A

COMPANIES THAT USE SIX SIGMA	
United States Army	N/A
United States Marine Corps	N/A
United States Navy	N/A
UnitedHealth Group	$71.86 billion
	TOTAL: $1246.81 Billion

This is just a partial list of the companies who use Six Sigma for their company's efficiency, and the list amounts to $1.25 trillion.

From all of this, you can see that Six Sigma is all about minimizing mistakes and maximizing value. This definition then causes many comparisons to Total Quality Management, another business efficiency practice, so it is best to address this and determine how the two practices differ.

Six Sigma As Opposed to Total Quality Management

As a result of Six Sigma being a new and revolutionary management practice, it has drawn comparisons to another management practice, which has been around for quite awhile: Total Quality Management.

Naturally, some criticize Six Sigma as being a copy of Total Quality Management, but this is not the case at all, and the two management forms are quite different.

Total Quality Management is a management strategy aimed at embedding awareness of quality in all organizational processes. It has been used widely through several industries, including manufacturing, education, government, and service industries, and also in the National Aeronautics and Space Association (NASA). It essentially operates under the concept of everyone in the organization working to create customer satisfaction and lower costs. This does sound like Six Sigma, but that is all that is similar.

Total Quality Management operates on three principles:

- Total: This involves the entire organization, from the supply chain to the product life cycle.

- Quality: This is the quality of the product or service that is provided to the customer.

- Management: This is the system of managing steps that include planning, organizing, controlling, leading, staffing, provisioning, and more.

Created by Armand Feigenbaum in his 1951 book *Quality Control: Principles, Practice and Administration*, in a chapter titled "Total Quality Control." this sparked the interest of many other business individuals, who fine-tuned it and turned it into the Total Quality Management concept that is used today.

Before delving further into this topic, take a look at the concept of DMAIC. This will be addressed later in an entire section, but having a basic understanding of the concept of DMAIC will help you through the coming chapters.

- Define: This is knowing the goals of the improvement strategy.

- Measure: This is looking at the current system and measuring its success rate.

- Analyze: This is looking at ways to eliminate the gap between the current performance of the system and desired goals.

- Improve: This is improving the system to get it to the Six Sigma level of efficiency.

- Control: This is controlling the new system and ensuring it stays at the Six Sigma level.

Why Your Business Needs Six Sigma

The book has defined Six Sigma and what it can do for a company, but why does your business truly need Six Sigma? Can it not just implement the strategies on its own and push the employees of the company to creating a peak level of efficiency?

The truth is you can try, but without the incredibly efficient organizational benefits of Six Sigma, you may be doomed to failure.

Six Sigma has proven itself to be highly effective throughout the past 20 years, with the largest companies in the world implementing and benefiting from it. You saw the chart that showed these companies, but what about the success stories related to them? Here are just a few of the success stories from companies that have used Six Sigma to their advantage.

- General Electric saw its profit rise from $7 billion to $10 billion due to Six Sigma, in only five years. That is an increase of $600,000,000 per year.

- DuPont increased its bottom line by $1 billion within two years of starting the Six Sigma program. Within four years, that number had shot up to $2.4 billion.

- The Bank of America was able to save hundreds of millions within three years of starting the Six Sigma program. In addition, they cut cycle times by half and reduced the number processing errors significantly.

- Honeywell achieved operating margins and savings of more than $2 billion in direct costs, a record for them, after implementing the program.

- Motorola, the guys who started it all, saved $2.2 billion in four years.

Now, why has it proven to be so popular among managers who use Six Sigma? Simply put, it delivers big-time results, and nothing makes managers happier than high efficiency and productivity coupled with extremely high customer satisfaction.

Here are reasons why managers of the world's largest companies have latched onto the Six Sigma program.

1. Clear Value Proposition and Return on Investment

    Six Sigma depends significantly on the unwavering focus on business Return on Investment. When done properly, Six Sigma can improve the characteristic of a business by more than 70 percent, which then causes more efficient operation procedures in the business, which then increases the value of the business in what it provides to its customers.

2. Top Commitment and Accountability

    The initiative of Six Sigma begins at the top, and the leadership of a company must be completely on board with the Six Sigma program through implementing plans and setting goals for everyone. This then makes management teams accountable for the performance of those goals, which they have set for their organizations and business groups.

3. Customer Focus

The business of Six Sigma is to drive a company's processes though the customers' requirements. Without the customers and the understanding of their requirements, no operations, processes, or improvements can be completed successfully. A company needs to understand what the customers need, what they want, and what they are willing to buy. Those managers that use Six Sigma quickly begin to understand that meeting the requirements of the customers is what makes the business strong and profitable.

4. Connected Business Metrics

Six Sigma focuses on measuring performance improvements, the finances of the business, and also operational improvements. To make this happen, the company's Six Sigma management system must include performance measures that are accessible and visible to everyone in the organization.

5. Process Orientation

By definition, Six Sigma improves all processes and their performances in a business. No matter the business or work, the performance of the design, characterization, optimization, and validation of processes must be the focal point of any Six Sigma program.

6. Project Focus

The Six Sigma project is how processes and systems are characterized and optimized. The leaders of the program

Introduction

will look at the opportunities for improvement with Six Sigma and assign the right Six Sigma specialists to complete them.

Many companies will feel that Three Sigma may be good enough. After all, you have 93 percent efficiency rate in terms of defects, which is excellent, so why waste the time, energy, and money on getting to Six Sigma, only for an extra 6 percent of efficiency and productivity?

This is a valid question, and it comes up when companies are wondering why they should implement Six Sigma.

The truth is that there is an exceptional reason for it, and this table shows you that while you may think your efficiency is high, 6 percent is a big gap that can seriously affect customer satisfaction.

**Note: These statistics are not accurate and are being used to show easily how much of a difference 6 percent makes.

QUANTITY OF PRODUCT	THREE SIGMA (93.379 PERCENT)	SIX SIGMA (99.99966 PERCENT)	DIFFERENCE
Each day, 2,000,000 pieces of mail go through the postal service.	This amounts to a total of 132,420 lost pieces of mail each day.	This amounts to seven lost pieces of mail per day.	132,413 lost pieces of mail each day.
Each month, 400,000 surgeries are performed.	Each month, there are a total of 26,484 surgeries done that result in serious complications.	Each month, there is one surgery that results in serious complications for the patient.	26,483 surgeries that result in serious complications.

QUANTITY OF PRODUCT	THREE SIGMA (93.379 PERCENT)	SIX SIGMA (99.99966 PERCENT)	DIFFERENCE
Each day, 9,000,000 pieces of baggage are processed in airports around the world.	Each day, a total of 595,890 bags are lost in airports around the world.	Each day, a total of three bags are lost in airports around the world.	585,887 bags lost in airports around the world in one day.
Each year, there are 10,000,000 flights around the world.	Each year, 662,00 flights have complications that endanger the lives of passengers on the plane.	Each year, 34 flights have complications that endanger the lives of passengers on the plane.	662,066 flights with complications that endanger the lives of passengers on the plane.
Each year, 330,000,000 toys are made with various materials.	Each year, 21,849,300 toys are sent out with defects that could cause harm to children.	Each year, 1,122 toys are sent out that could cause harm to children.	21,848,178 toys sent out each year that could cause harm to children.

Just with these five examples, you can see how much of a difference Three Sigma is from Six Sigma, even if it is just 6 percent. That 6 percent is the difference between life and death for thousands, if not millions, of people in these examples. Six percent makes a huge difference, and that is why Six Sigma is something every single business should look at in its organization.

How This Book Is Organized

This book is organized into a series of seven sections, which address different areas of Six Sigma and how it can benefit your company. The first section focuses on Six Sigma, with an overview of its history, the language used, the formula for success, and how to conduct Six Sigma modeling.

The second section focuses on Six Sigma leadership, including determining if you are ready for Six Sigma and how managers and Six Sigma go together. The Six Sigma team, including explanations of black, green, and master black belts is addressed, as is team training.

Section Three goes into DMAIC and shows the what and the how, and also the tools of defining, measuring, analyzing, improving, and controlling.

Section Four looks at DMADV and the what, the how, and the tools of defining, measuring, analyzing, designing, and verifying.

Section Five is about Lean Six Sigma, its principles, and how to become a lean business. Kaizen Methodology and how Lean Six Sigma affects small product-based businesses and small service-based businesses are also discussed.

Section Six will look at the other Six Sigma Models, including MAIC, DCCDI, DCDOV, DMADOV, IDOV, and CDOC.

The last section, Section Seven, will look at the Six Sigma Toolkit at your disposal, including the Failure Modes and Effects Analysis, Goodness of Fit Tests, and Exponentially Weighted Moving Averages.

Conclusion

Across the world, the largest companies on Earth have implemented Six Sigma methodology in their organization in an effort to increase customer satisfaction, profits, and productivity through the most efficient means possible. Six Sigma is a revolutionary concept because when completed successfully, it allows for as little as a 3.4 per one million-unit defect rate, which is astounding, as you have seen.

Yet, Six Sigma is much more; it is a business philosophy that is literally changing how business is done and how companies interact with their customers. It is changing the world of business because it is pushing the message that the customers are the key to business, and without proper customer satisfaction, all profit is lost.

When you look at the graph comparing Three Sigma and Six Sigma, you can see how important customer satisfaction plays into the concept. A total of 595,890 lost bags of luggage every day means 595,890 angry customers and 595,890 customers who may not use that particular airline company again. This can mean the loss of billions of dollars for the airline industry as a result. Although, when the airline industry operates on a Six Sigma model that means only three bags lost each day, out of nine million bags. A loss of three bags each day adds up to only three angry customers, and instead of billions lost to the airline industry, the loss culminates into a few thousand dollars. That is immaterial because the millions of satisfied customers will more than make up the difference.

Using Six Sigma is about gaining high profits through excellent customer service that comes from better efficiency with products and services. This is a revolutionary concept and it is little wonder why it has become so popular around the world.

Think about it: The largest companies in the world have seen their profits increase by not millions, but billions of dollars through the use of Six Sigma. If it can do that for their organization, just think about what it can do for yours.

Section 1

Six Sigma Overview

"Quality in a product or service is not what the supplier puts in. It is what the customer gets out and is willing to pay for. A product is not quality because it is hard to make and costs a lot of money, as manufacturers typically believe."

-Peter Drucker

Section Introduction

Despite being a relatively foreign concept to many individuals, Six Sigma is something that can be easily understood by nearly everyone who comes across it. It may take time, but you can know why Six Sigma is perfect for your company and why you should care about the things it can do for you.

Through this section, you will be addressing the various aspects of basic Six Sigma, including where it came from and how it has changed the world of business immeasurably. Through this chapter, you will learn about Six Sigma and why it focuses on customers. You will also learn its terminology and the processes that it takes to make your business a Six Sigma company.

As revealed in the previous section, it is important that a customer not settle to be a Three Sigma company. Whenever a company can, it needs to shoot to be Six Sigma, because a 3.4 out of one million defect rate is astonishingly low, and every company needs to push for it.

Six Sigma is something that the largest companies in the world have taken as a management practice, but many smaller organizations seem to neglect or forget about it. They choose not to implement it; possibly thinking it is something for large companies and not small ones.

The truth is that if you have employees, Six Sigma is for you. Whether it is 10 employees or 10,000 employees, you can improve your company's performance and the customer satisfaction that drives your sales by implementing Six Sigma.

Section 1: Six Sigma Overview

In terms of business, Six Sigma is extremely recent, only coming to light in the past 22 years. Even after it was created in 1986, it still took a few years before companies began to take notice and implement themselves.

The point of this section is to show you that Six Sigma is for everyone, and by changing your practices and implementing new solutions and processes for your company, you, too, can benefit from being a Six Sigma company.

The Six Sigma Manual

Chapter 1
The Innovation of Six Sigma

"Great discoveries and improvements invariably involve the cooperation of many minds. I may be given credit for having blazed the trail, but when I look at the subsequent developments, I feel the credit is due to others rather than to myself."

- Alexander Graham Bell

Six Sigma was a revolutionary concept when it first emerged in the 1980s, but like any revolutionary concept, it took awhile before it caught on, and many people wondered about the feasibility of such a method of business. As with anything that was too good to be ignored, it gradually began to take hold. Soon enough, it had become one of the top ways many companies were able to increase their efficiency and productivity while improving customer satisfaction, which then translated into increased sales and revenue for that company.

Six Sigma is something that did not come out of nowhere. Isaac Newton once said the only reason he could see further than anyone else, in terms of science, was because he stood on the shoulders of giants; this is exactly true in Six Sigma. The creators and implementers of this revolutionary business strategy used the concepts of prominent businessmen and businesswomen in the past to create their own contribution to the world of business. The reason they were able to create such a revolutionary concept such as Six Sigma was because they stood on the shoulders of business giants of the past and pushed things a little further by combining what they knew and what they wanted to do.

This is the case with any revolutionary concept. Look at the inventions in the world around us. The telegraph created the telephone, which created the radio, which created the television, which helped to create the computer, which created the Internet. Everything that has been created has been a variation or improvement on the item before it. This is because people can look at the radio and think "It sends voices over the air, so why can't we send images as well?" This then creates the possibility of advancement and improvement. Six Sigma is no different, and companies are saving millions of dollars because they ask those same questions. They improve on what they have by finding out what the customers want. This is a continuous process that allows them to become leaders of industry and the world's largest revenue-generating companies.

So, where did Six Sigma come from? To find out, travel back to the crazy, Me-Decade of the 1980s.

Six Sigma arose during a time when the executives, engineering, and manufacturing, at Motorola were just awakening to the need. The change began in the 1970s for Motorola, when a Motorola factory where Quasar televisions were manufactured was sold to a Japanese firm, Matsushita. New ways of operating the factory were put in place, and under the Japanese management system, the factory was producing television sets with a fraction

Chapter 1: The Innovation of Six Sigma

of the defects they had produced before. This provided an eye-opening picture: leadership directly influences the quality of products. During the 1979 annual Motorola officers meeting, Vice President Art Sundry said: "Our quality stinks".

Against this backdrop, statistical methods started "rising from the ashes," like the mythical Phoenix bird in the sites of Motorola in Phoenix, Arizona. Some engineers attended classes on Design of Experiments, and the very first statistical experiment, by Darlene Justus, Eric Maass, and J. Ronald Lawson, led to removing a dozen non-value added steps in the process, reducing the cycle time for the special semiconductors to a fifth of what it had been before. These special semiconductors were used in satellites, and before this first experiment, the cycle times had threatened to delay satellite launches. Also, using statistical methods for other products tripled yields from about 25 percent to 75 percent almost overnight.

These dramatic results were noticed by Motorola engineers and managers, and a network of statistics users formed in 1980. This informal network shared success stories, problems, and solutions, and started brainstorming similarities among the successes toward developing a common method. Growing interest led to the development of internal courses on statistical methods and bringing in external consultants for training classes, coordinated by Janet Fiero, who was responsible for training in the Phoenix area.

By 1982, the success stories and statistical classes were being recognized across Motorola. Executives and managers started hiring experts on statistical methods, either as full-time employees or as consultants, including Dr. Mikel Harry, Mario Perez-Wilson, and Harrison "Skip" Weed, Professors Dennis Young and Douglas Montgomery.

Janet Fiero was promoted to Motorola Corporate Director of Motorola Training and Education Center at Motorola's headquarters in Chicago. She strongly promoted statistics training throughout Motorola. These classes captured the imagination of a senior engineer named Bill Smith. Bill Smith worked on field failures — products that would fail after people bought and started to use them.

Smith's key insight was to relate the failures of products he dealt with as a quality manager to product properties that were margins — just on the edge of missing customer expectations. Smith realized the probability of having an early life failure was compounded if there were many components.

From what he had learned from the classes, Smith reasoned if the product was designed and manufactured with a tight distribution, few parts would be near the edge of missing customer expectations, then many good things would happen: customer failures would disappear and manufacturing yields would increase.

To make his point, with Motorola's management aware of the success of Matsushita manufacturing higher quality Quasar television sets from the former Motorola manufacturing line, Smith gathered benchmarking data on yields of Japanese TV sets and determined we could have several thousand components and get high, 99 percent yields, if the critical characteristics had distributions that were so tight they were six standard deviations away from the customer requirements. From that insight arose the name, Six Sigma!

Chapter 1: The Innovation of Six Sigma

According to the recollections of Motorola's CEO, Bob Galvin:

"… Bill Smith called me asking for an appointment. He came to my office and explained the theory of latent defects. I called him back the next day to try to better understand what he was talking about. He soon became a sophisticated advisor in applying statistical methods to improve quality."

Smith had completed the most critical step — achieving Executive Engagement. In 1986, with CEO Bob Galvin's backing, the Six Sigma concept was communicated top-down and accepted throughout Motorola. On January 15, 1987, Motorola officially launched and announced Six Sigma and set the Six Sigma goal: achieving less than 3.4 defects per million opportunities.

In 1988, Motorola won the very first Malcolm Baldridge National Quality Award, given by the U.S. Congress to recognize and inspire the pursuit of quality in American business. Shortly thereafter, a very proud Bob Galvin announced his willingness to share what we had developed and learned:

"…we will share Six Sigma with the world, and it will come back to us…with new ideas and new perspectives…."

In 1989, Motorola established the Six Sigma Research Institute in Chicago. Other companies joined within the next year, including IBM, TI, Westinghouse, and Kodak.

For Motorola executives, it was not hard to switch to this new method of management. A quick look at what other companies contend with who do not use Six Sigma shows them they made the right choice.

Companies that operate at only three or four sigma spend 25 to 40 percent of their revenue fixing problems. This is the cost of quality, or the cost of poor quality. In contrast, Six Sigma companies like Motorola spend less than 5 percent of their revenue to fix problems. It has been estimated that the difference between Three/Four Sigma and Six Sigma companies is $8 billion to $12 billion.

Process Improvement

Early on, Six Sigma became known for process improvement and its process improvement teams. These were the individuals and groups who would look at the current situation in the company and begin to devise ways to improve the process to make higher efficiency, higher customer satisfaction, and a better understanding of how everything works.

To help manage this, Motorola created process improvement teams. These are teams that are focused on improving a specific process, which could be quality, cost, customer satisfaction, and more. The thing that sets these teams apart is that they focus on the entire process, rather than just on a particular aspect of that process. Motorola understood early on that a process is just an integrated chain of activities that add value to a product or service. For example, when a company is making a car, the process could be defined as having a beginning of getting the parts and an ending of shipping the car to the dealership.

Process improvement teams work both on improvement and radical change. They are able to do this because they are made up of members who have worked in the process on a constant basis and have a thorough understanding of how it works. When they are part of a team, they are like a multicultural society. Where the multicultural society has different ethnicities, religions, and traditions, the team is made up of employees from the company who have different bosses, different experiences, and are in different levels of the company's hierarchy.

Without process improvement teams, the entire concept of Six Sigma falls apart and companies will fall back into being Two-, Three-, or Four-Sigma companies. As a result, it is extremely important that process improvement teams are put together properly to ensure the most cooperation and highest level of efficiency measures possible.

Customer Focus

Customer focus is easy to define; it is simply the concept the customer is the only person qualified to specify what quality means. This then causes companies to have detailed analyses of who the customers are, what their needs are, what they want, how they rate the products and services compared with competitors, and how to keep the customers satisfied.

Simply put, when customer requirements are assessed, the estimates of customer needs must then be replaced by real customer needs. Companies often discover that what they believed about customers was quite wrong, and they suddenly become aware that cost savings and the improvement of relations with customers comes through proper understanding of the needs of the customer.

When a company is looking at the customer or focusing on them, they need to consider everything about them and the product they use, including the design, use, delivery, and billing. They need to be all-encompassing as to what the customer wants, because only by knowing what your customer wants, inside and out, will the company be able to be successful in its Six Sigma goals.

Whenever detailed specifications come from a customer, the customer will then become the focus of the company. When the focus is on the customer, exciting levels of quality can be delivered through innovations. One of the greatest examples of a company focusing on itself, rather than its customers, is Polaroid. For years, the company focused on becoming more efficient without taking into consideration the needs of the customer. While they were doing this, the customers began to switch over to digital cameras, leaving Polaroid's products in the dust and part of a bygone era. As a result, Polaroid filed for Chapter 11 bankruptcy on October 11, 2001, with all of the company's assets sold to Bank One. The company was then renamed Polaroid Corporation, and in 2007, it stopped making Polaroid cameras, while in 2009, it will stop making Polaroid film.

Failure to know what customers want means the company will eventually be lost in the changing tides of technology and customer interests. With customer focus through Six Stigma, certain questions are asked:

- What does the customer want?
- What is the customer looking for in the future of the product?
- What are the trends the customer is following?
- How much does the customer want to spend?
- What innovations does the customer want?

These are by no means the only things asked by companies looking to focus on the customer, but they are the most important. There is an excellent example of this in the book Moment of Truth, written by Jan Carlzon, the former president of SAS Airlines.

"An individual without information can't take responsibility. An individual with information can't help but take responsibility."

- Jan Carlzon

During the 1970s and early 1980s, SAS Airlines was in a tailspin, no pun intended. It was losing money as the airline market changed considerably due to deregulation. As a result, many airlines were cutting costs, especially in the realm of employees, where many were laid off as a result. Although, instead of doing this, SAS Airlines, under Jan Carlzon's leadership, decided to become known as the No. 1 business traveler's airline. As a result, every expense and resource in the company was evaluated for how it would contribute to the satisfaction of the business customer. Entire departments and processes were dropped to make way for new operations and procedures. While at the same time, anything that helped the business traveler was expanded, so the money saved was put into expanding this part of the business. Instead of cutting costs as they lost money, they spent $45 million on customer service to improve punctuality and service quality. As a result, the company reversed its money-losing trend and instead began to make money through improved customer satisfaction.

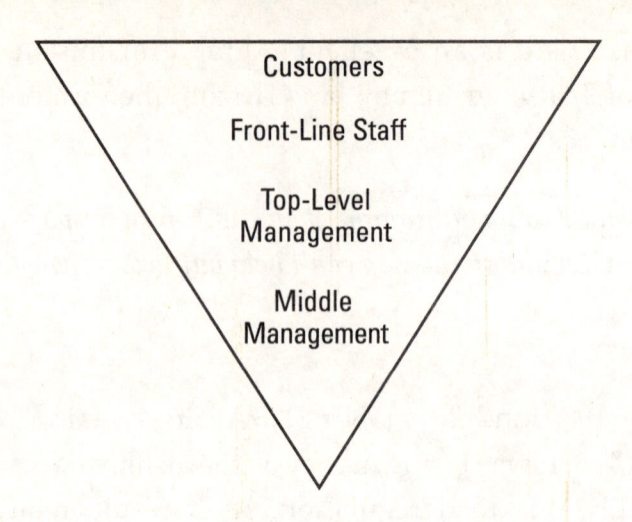

```
        ▽
   Customers
  Front-Line Staff
  Top-Level
  Management
  Middle
  Management
```

As can be seen in the figure, the organizational model of the Six Sigma company differs from the traditional type, with top management on top, making the decisions. For a Six Sigma company, it is the customers who make the decisions as to the direction of the company, because the customers are the ones who know what they want out of the company.

Conclusion

The first chapter concludes with the understanding of where Six Sigma came from. To review, Six Sigma came along because someone, in particular Bill Smith, asked, "Why can't we improve service and quality?" He asked these questions because he knew the customer drives the economy and the business, and if you do not take into consideration what the customer wants, you are in serious danger of being left behind and lost. Polaroid is a perfect example of this, as they did not see the market changing and they lost out because of it. They are not the only company, but at the same time, other companies have seen the market change because they have looked at what the customers want and they have adjusted to it. They have worked to create exactly what the customer is looking for and have managed to improve themselves as a result.

An excellent example of this is Apple®. They were once one of the leading computer companies in the world, but poor management and ineffective products through the late 1980s and early 1990s resulted in the company nearly disappearing. Yet, they adjusted and began to look at what customers were looking for. As a result, by the 2000s, they had changed and become one of the top computer companies again, offering the best-selling computer products of the past 50 years, including the iPhone® and iPod®. This is an example of a company knowing what is around the corner because they knew to ask the customers what they wanted.

For any company to survive in our current age of marketing and quickly shifting customer views, they have to put the customers on top and understand what the customers are going to be attracted to in the future. Companies have to put the customer first, and they have to shift their marketing strategies and concepts accordingly. They have to stop thinking about improving their efficiency inside without improving their efficiency outside the company as well. For a company to survive properly, it is all about the customer and what the customer wants.

If your company chooses to focus only on itself, without thinking about the customer, efficiency, or productivity, then you can join Polaroid in the graveyard of once-successful companies. On the other hand, if you want to progress further with Six Sigma and become the envy of your sector, then move forward with Motorola and Apple to become a leader.

Six Sigma is not a hard concept; it is essentially focusing on the customer and understanding that with no customer satisfaction, there is no profit, and with no profit comes no responsibility to run the company, because you will not have one.

Now, move on to understanding Six Sigma lingo.

Chapter 2
The Language of Six Sigma

"We begin life with the world presenting itself to us as it is. Someone — our parents, teachers, analysts — hypnotizes us to 'see' the world and construe it in the 'right' way. These others label the world, attach names and give voices to the beings and events in it, so that thereafter, we cannot read the world in any other language or hear it saying other things to us. The task is to break the hypnotic spell, so that we become undeaf, unblind, and multilingual, thereby letting the world speak to us in new voices and write all its possible meanings in the new book of our existence. Be careful in your choice of hypnotists."

-Sidney Jourard

Six Sigma may be something that can be easily understood, at least the concept behind it, but understanding the terminology and language of Six Sigma is a completely different story. In this case, you have to look at the most obscure forms of mathematics and statistical reasoning to get a firm grasp on the fundamentals of Six Sigma.

This chapter addresses the key terms that apply to all of the Six Sigma methodologies, and you will learn about the meanings of common statistical terms, including:

- Critical to X (CTX)

- Critical to Quality (CTQ)

- Design of Experiments (DOE)

- Gage R&R

- Internal Rate of Return (IRR)

- Metrics

- Voice of the Customer (VOC)

- Defects per Million Opportunities (DPMO)

- Performance Variation

- Performance Specifications

- Process Input

- Process Output

- SIPOC

Knowing what these terms mean will help you understand how you can apply Six Sigma to your company. If you fail to understand the terms behind Six Sigma, you will most likely fall behind and become a Three or Four Sigma company, which have shown to be quite ineffective, despite the plus-90 percent effectiveness.

Many of the concepts here are part of any business training, but have simply been modified to fit the Six Sigma methodologies. Most are quite easy to understand — some are not — but they are all critical to ensuring your Six Sigma goals are met and your company remains profitable and viable into the future.

Critical to X

Looking at this figure, it is understandable if you have little or no idea what it means. Most do not, but do not worry; everything will be explained to you.

In Six Sigma, all the important characteristics are referred to as Critical to X, or more specifically, CTXs. In this, C stands for Critical, T stands for To and X Represents what the characteristic is linked to, be it cost, time, satisfaction, or something else. You can use a graph to represent the target values of any CTX quite easily.

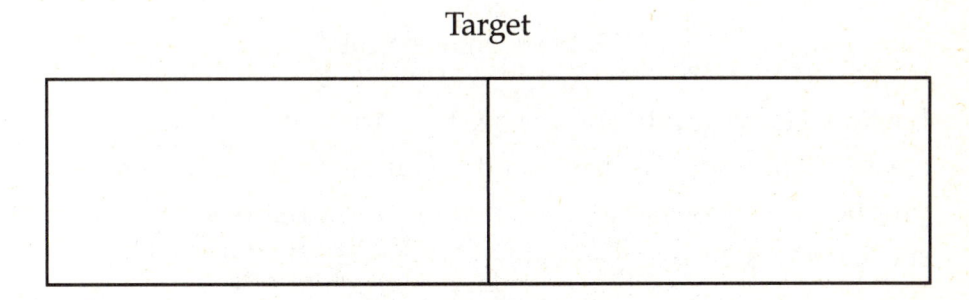

Target

CTX Performance Scale

In this graph, the performance scale is expressed in units such as time or size. You want to come as close as you can to your performance target. This is a significant point in Six Sigma, because the closer you are to your performance target, the higher your efficiency will be. Remember, to be Six Sigma, you have to be upwards of 99.99966 percent efficiency.

Of course, no matter how hard you try, even with Six Sigma, it is nearly impossible to hit your target value perfectly every single time. You will get close, but variations will happen.

Every time a product comes off the line, it will be different from previous instances and products coming off of that same line. It may be a difference in texture, quality, and the time it takes to make it, but something small will be different.

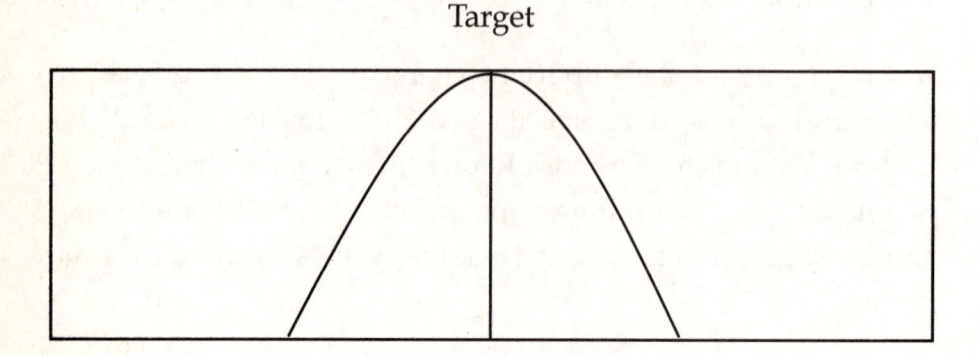

Target

CTX Performance Scale

Looking at this graph, you can see the variations in products will create a bell curve. To help limit the amount of variations on a product, it is possible to set limits on the variations and put in specifications that can be deemed acceptable for the product.

As a result of this, it is possible to accept the presence of deviations or variations, while not ignoring the tendency to create defects and cause business loss, no matter how small that may be.

Look at the graph again, with the lower and upper limits of acceptability for deviations outlined. These limits help give parameters for defining, measuring, analyzing, improving, and controlling the quality of a service or product that a company puts out.

Chapter 2: The Language of Six Sigma

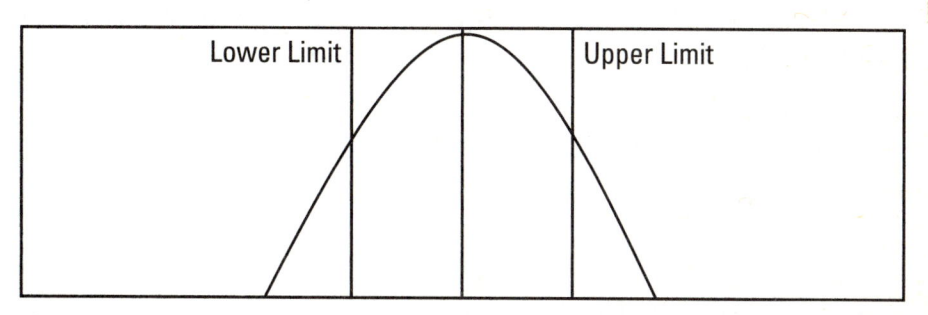

Target

CTX Performance Scale

As can be seen, the lower and upper limits are now defined on the graph, and anything falling outside of that is termed defective and not released to the public.

Examples of this include:

- A pizza delivery company pledging to have all pizzas delivered between 15 and 30 minutes

- A computer company that pledges there will be no more than one defective computer for every 2,000 made

- An insurance company that pledges to process all orders within one week of the application being completed

- A car company pledging that a defect in the engine will not affect more than 1 out of 10,000 cars produced

This then allows companies to set certain guidelines for itself. For the pizza delivery company, if the pizza arrives 40 minutes after it was ordered, the customer is given a discount. This then allows the customer to feel happy at the discount, making them forget about the pizza being ten minutes late, which then creates customer satisfaction.

A computer company knows that if 10 out of 100, or 10 percent, of all the computers made through them are defective, and they sell 100,000 computers that year, that means 10,000 angry customers, who tell 40,000 other people about the poor quality of the computers. That equates to millions of dollars of lost revenue for the company.

The insurance company knows that if an order is over one week, customers get irate. They know this because they asked the customer; therefore, keeping the wait time for the customer down to one week keeps the customer happy.

The car company knows this defect in the engine will occur after 60,000 miles, which is outside the warranty of the customer. As a result, they deem only 1 out of 10,000 cars can have this defect. That is a percentage of about .01 percent, or 2,000 customers if 200,000 of those cars are sold. Anything higher, and they risk losing business.

Critical to Quality

Critical to Quality, or CTQ, is the key measurable characteristics of a product or process, which has performance standards or specific limits that must be met to satisfy the customer. This will align improvements to designs with the requirements of the customer.

They also represent the product or service characteristic that the customer defines, which can include the upper and lower specification limits or other factors that are related to putting out an acceptable product or service with a low rate of defects.

To clarify, CTQs are what the customer expects from the product you are putting out. They are the needs of the customer and can be expressed in plain English, and it is the company that needs to convert what the customer wants into measurable terms using the various tools of Six Sigma.

One key component to having successful CTQs is the elimination, or reduction of variation. It is exceedingly important that variations are kept to a minimum when you want to meet a customer's Critical to Quality requirement. To eliminate variation, you use the Define-Measure-Analyze-Improve-Control (DMAIC) model (more on this later) and other tools to make the decisions that will eliminate variations, which are driven by data.

There are many examples of companies that do not think about the Critical to Quality requirements the customer sets out, and this causes them to suffer horribly. Here is a good hypothetical example.

SUV Company A is one of the leaders in the manufacture of SUVs. They have been in business for 20 years and have sold millions of SUVs around the world. They have been incredibly popular, and owning one of their SUVs is a sign of status. SUV Company B is also a leader in the manufacturing of SUVs and has been doing it for just as long as SUV Company A. They are well regarded, and millions of their product have been sold around the world.

As the two companies begin to move into the second decade of the 21st century, they notice that sales are beginning to drop on their by-and-large incredibly popular SUV lines. SUV Company A does not hear the customer requirements or care much for them. Their Chief Executive Officer thinks "customers do not decide the course of the company; management does." As a result, they begin to focus more on fine-tuning the vehicles for safety, thinking customers worry about the safety of the vehicles, while at the same time improving the space inside.

SUV Company B, conversely, does several customer surveys and also polls their current customers to find out what they want out of their SUV and also why they may choose not to buy an SUV. As a result of this, they find the customers are worried about the record high gas prices and are choosing to buy cars that are hybrids or have exceptional gas mileage. So, SUV Company B decides to shift gears and begins releasing hybrid SUVs and SUVs with extremely high gas mileage. They soon begin to see their sales improve as a result.

Five years later, SUV Company A is out of business and SUV Company B is one of the leading SUV manufacturers in the entire world.

From this example, you can see that not listening to customers, or choosing not to ask them, results in bad business, poor customer satisfaction, low sales, and future problems.

Asking customers what they want can fix a lot of problems. Remember Polaroid? If they had asked their customers what they wanted, they may have shifted their focus to digital camera products, rather than staying with 36mm film. Knowing what your customers want and putting those solutions in place is key to a company surviving.

Design of Experiments

The quick definition of Design of Experiments (DOE) is that it is a structured and organized method to determine the relationship between two or more factors that affect a process and the output of the process. It can also be defined as conducting and analyzing controlled tests to determine which of the factors have the largest effects on the output, and understand how the important factors affect the output.

With a clear understanding of that, Six Sigma is much easier.

To help you understand the concept, begin by looking at the types of variables you will deal with.

- Response Variable — This is the variable that is being investigated and can also be called the dependent variable or the output.

- Primary Variables or control factors — The controllable variables believed to have the most effect. They can be things like temperature, pressure speed, vendor, product method, or operator.

- Background Variables or Noise factors — These are variables that may have an effect on the experiment, but cannot be manipulated. The effect of that could contaminate the primary variable effects, unless it is handled properly.

- Experiment Error — Noise factors like temperature, humidity changes, and measurement error can be sources of variation. These represent the experimental error of the process, and the effects should be kept from contaminating the primary variable's effects by randomization (doing the tests or runs in the experiment in a random order).

- Interaction — This is where the effect of one factor on the response depends on the level of another factor — like the ease of using a match to start a campfire depends on how wet the wood is.

Now that variables and definitions have been addressed, characteristics of design experiments will be covered.

There are three things that a good experiment plan depends on:

- The purpose of the experiment

- Physical restrictions on the process of taking measurements

- Restrictions imposed by limitations of time, money, material, and personnel

There are two other concepts that are also extremely important when someone is doing Design of Experiments, particularly a Six Sigma analyst.

- Replication — This is the collection of more than one observation of the same run, or settings of the factors. This allows the experimenter to estimate the experiment error.

- Randomization — To eliminate any sort of bias in the experiment, it is important that the effects of noise factors aren't confused with the effects of control factors. If, for example, the tests with more of a control factor, like the amount of salt, are run as the day gets hotter, then you could confuse the effect of temperature with the effect of salt. Randomization changes the order so that sometimes high levels of salt are run earlier and sometimes later in the day.

There are six steps to the DOE.

1. Define the problem: You need to define the nature of the problem in quantitative terms.

2. Define the objectives: Be certain that the experiment is focused on getting specific results and useful information.

Chapter 2: The Language of Six Sigma 55

3. Design the experiment: Use the DOE tools to design the experiment that will satisfy your objectives.

4. Carefully perform the experiment, with the runs in a randomized order.

5. Analyze the results of the experiment, and determine which factors have a significant effect on the response.

6. Make decisions based on your results, and devise a plan that will help you meet your objectives.

Gage Repeatability and Reproducibility is a tool that measures the amount of variation in the measurement that arises from the measurement device and the people taking the measurement. This is frequently reported as a percentage of tolerance or as a percentage of the total process variation.

When it is expressed as a percentage of tolerance, it indicates the usefulness of the gage system by determining how much the measurement system affects part acceptance. Tolerance is calculated as the upper specification limit minus the lower specification limit. If the measurement system contributes too much to the variation of the measurement, then you might incorrectly throw away good parts, or incorrectly accept bad parts based on the measurement error.

When Gage R&R is expressed as a percentage of process variation, it indicates the usefulness of the gage system for use in charting and process capability analysis.

Decisions about whether the measurement system is acceptable are based on either a percentage of tolerance or percentage of the total process variation is as follows:

- 0 to 10 percent: Acceptable

- 10 to 30 percent: Fair

- Above 30 percent: Unacceptable

Internal Rate of Return

This is the equivalent interest that would be gained by the project if the net present value of the cash flow was invested in a certain time period. Using the Internal Rate of Return allows the company to compare projects with higher Internal Rate of Returns associated with projects that are providing a lower return.

It is important to determine in the financial analysis of projects just how much of a yield an investment in a project has with a given price and cash flows; many companies will prioritize their projects based on this and perhaps compare the yield you would get putting the same cash into a bank or Certificate of Deposit. A good example of this is as follows:

A quality control group at a local computer company found there is a problem with lost computer tools. Through research, they have found that in the rush to provide fast service to customers, many tools get misplaced and lost, which then causes problems with turnaround times for employees as they either look for the lost tools or share them. As a result, the group finds that if the computer company invests in a $3,500 sensor system that will be able to alert when a tool has left a certain prescribed zone around a table, they can eliminate this problem and the cost of constantly buying new tools that get misplaced, stolen, or accidentally thrown away in the trash. They have found that after five years, the system can be sold again for $1,000. Buying this sensor will save the following amounts:

YEAR	SAVINGS
1	$500
2	$750
3	$1,000
4	$1,250
5	$1,500

Looking at the data, you can determine the Internal Rate of Return with the following chart:

f(x) = IRR (D3:D8)

C	D
YEAR	CASH FLOW
0	($3,500)
1	$500
2	$750
3	$1,000
4	$1,250
5	$2,500
	16%

In the last year — year five — you can add the $1,000 sale of the equipment to the cash flow. The initial investment is $3,500, added cash flow within five years is $6,000, and the return equals $2,500 return on investment. Using a spreadsheet like Excel with the IRR (Internal Rate of Return) function can show that the internal rate of return would be about 16 percent.

Metrics

Metrics are essentially what are used to measure and understand quality levels. The word metric means measurement (remember the metric system?), so the word is used in an organization to measure how well it is doing in meeting its customers' expectations, and its own business expectations.

There are attributes to good metrics, and they are as follows:

- They are centered on the customer and focused on the indicators that will provide value to customers, including quality, reliability, responsiveness, and delivery time.

- They measure performance over a given time.

- They are linked with the mission, strategies, and actions of the organization.

- They are developed cooperatively by teams of people, who put together the data by collecting and processing it.

Voice of the Customer

This is essentially what the customer wants. It is the process used to capture the requirements and feedback from the customers to provide them with the best-quality product or service. This process is especially important and proactive, with innovative new ways to capture the changing needs and wants of the customers over the course of time. The direct voice of the customer can be captured in a variety of means, including through surveys, customer interviews, focus groups, observation, warranty data, and complaint logs. Businesses will then use the voice of the customer to identify the attributes that are needed to supply component or material to improve the process or product.

Defects per Million Opportunities

This book has addressed defects per million opportunities and demonstrated that in a Six Sigma business, that defect rate is only 3.4 defects per million opportunities. Essentially, you find the defects per million opportunities by multiplying the defects by 1,000,000, and dividing by the number of units measured times the number of opportunities for error or ways a defect can occur in a unit, which then gives you the average number of defects found over a million opportunities.

If a small company made toys that involved putting 5 parts together, each part representing an opportunity for error, and made 10 bad toys out of a thousand toys built, they would have 10 x 1 million / (1000 x 5), or 2000 defects per million opportunities.

SIPOC

Standing for Suppliers, Inputs, Process, Output, and Customers, SIPOC allows the business to obtain inputs from suppliers, add those to the process, and provide an output that meets or exceeds the needs and requirements of the customer.

This is one of the most important building blocks of the Six Sigma process, and with this book, companies can build their first controlled and organized view of the process that employees work by. Split up the word to understand what each part provides to this process:

- Suppliers: These are the people, organizations, and sources of the materials or information that are needed to be consumed or transformed in the process.

- Inputs: These are the materials and information that are provided through the suppliers, which will be consumed or transformed in the process.

- Process: This is the action that transforms inputs to outputs.

- Outputs: These are the products and services that are produced by the process and eventually used by the customer.

- Customers: These are the people, groups, and companies that use the output of the processes.

It is an easy concept, but an example will be presented to clarify.

Jersey Company in Anytown, USA, makes hockey jerseys for clients all over the world. To make these products, they need to go through a set series of actions that will create what the customer is looking for and hoping to buy.

1. Jersey Company contacts the people who provide them with the materials, including Fabric Company, Ink Company, and Thread Company.

2. Jersey Company buys their fabric from Fabric Company, the ink they need from Ink Company, and thread from Thread Company.

3. Jersey Company then processes the fabric into what they need, using the thread and the ink they have purchased from their suppliers.

4. Jersey Company outputs the jerseys that were made from fabric, ink, and thread to various retailers around the world.

5. Customers in particular cities come along and buy the jersey of their favorite team from a retailer that sells the jerseys Jersey Company makes.

As can be seen, there are steps to developing a SIPOC, which needs to be built from the inside-out, beginning in the center, with the process.

1. Identify the process that the company needs to define, including determining its scope and boundary points.

2. Identify the outputs, as in what the company will be releasing to the customers.

3. Define the types of customers who will buy the outputs that the company's processes produce.

4. Identify what the customers' requirements are and what they expect from the company and its services.

5. Define the inputs of the process, as in what materials need to go into the company to create the outputs it needs to satisfy the customers through the company's processes.

6. Find the suppliers or sources of those inputs.

As a result of this information, you need to ask certain questions to determine how best to fill in the gaps of the SIPOC.

1. What value does this create for the company?

2. What output is produced?

3. Who is the company that manages the process?

4. Who provides the inputs for the process?

5. What are those inputs?

6. What resources does the process need?

7. What steps create the value the company needs?

Conclusion

Understanding the concepts behind Six Sigma has a lot to do with understanding the terminology that has been covered in this chapter. While a lot of this terminology might seem difficult to understand and a bit foreign, you do not have to worry too much about being an expert in all of them. The point of this chapter was simply to help you get an understanding of the concepts behind how Six Sigma is created, implemented, and maintained. Understanding the terminology of this chapter will help you change your business from a Two or Three Sigma into a Six Sigma.

There are enough bits of information on different forms of terminology and how they apply to Six Sigma to fill several books, but that is not the point here. The point is not to make you a professor in Six Sigma, but simply to help you become a bit more adept at understanding what Six Sigma is and how it works.

Understanding the scientific method of Six Sigma and the Six Sigma formula is the next step.

Chapter 3
The Formula for Success

"You only have to do a very few things right in your life so long as you don't do too many things wrong."

Warren Buffett

Chapter Introduction

There is a scientific method to nearly everything that is done in our lives, and this is true in Six Sigma as well. The scientific method is used to understand Six Sigma. It is also used as our model of understanding.

Scientific method involves trial and error, figuring out what works and what does not, while attempting new variables and new elements to see what will happen. Civilization is founded on scientific method, and without it, you would be in the Dark Ages. Scientific method teaches to question what you see and determine how to make it better.

This is why it is so important in the world of Six Sigma, because it allows you to work to get to Six Sigma from Two, Three, or Four Sigma. It allows us to determine what will work and what will not.

There is a misconception that says Six Sigma is all about business, and while its role is in business, it has much to do with math and calculations. You have to use calculations, tests, and experiments to find out how things work for your company and what will work in the future. Through experiments, you determine what the customers will want and how to provide it to them.

This chapter is one of math and calculations, formulas, and scientific methods. This is not to say it is a hard chapter, but it is a different from your usual business concepts. It involves knowing more than just how business works and what the customer wants, so be prepared.

Using the Scientific Method to Understand Six Sigma

Scientific method essentially refers to the body of techniques that are used to investigate certain things, and also to acquire new knowledge and improve on previous knowledge. It is essentially based on gathering observational, empirical, and measurable evidence that is subjected to the principles of reasoning.

Normally, the entire scientific method begins with a hypothesis. This is a theory that the person or group running the scientific method process comes to and is attempting to prove. Then experimental studies are done to test out the hypothesis and either prove it right or wrong.

There are several important points to the scientific method, and one of the most important is that the process must be objective to reduce bias on the results. If there is a bias toward the results, it can change the results. For example, if an individual believes that man evolved from squirrels, not apes, then they may alter the elements and variables of the experiment to gain the results that they want, not the results as they truly are. To ensure there is no bias, the scientific method uses documentation, archiving, and sharing of data and methods to ensure that other individuals and groups can scrutinize it and make sure there is no bias. This is the full disclosure of the results.

The pioneer of scientific method is Ibn al-Haytham, who lived from 965 to 1039 and had a desire to find the truth. He once said:

"Truth is sought for its own sake. And those who are engaged upon the quest for anything for its own sake are not interested in other things. Finding the truth is difficult, and the road to it is rough."

There is a hypothetico-deductive model for scientific method that goes as follows:

1. Use experience to consider the problem and attempt to make sense of it. It is important to look at your previous explanations to determine how they affect your current results. If you have never done this experiment before, then skip this step.

2. Form a conjecture when there is nothing else known. Try to state your explanation or hypothesis in a manner that can be documented.

3. Deduce a prediction from that explanation; if step two is true, then what consequences will follow the results?

4. Test out your theory from the opposite side and try to disprove the conclusion you have come to. You need to make sure your theory or hypothesis stands up to your conclusions.

Nevertheless, understanding what the scientific method is does not help unless you look at how the scientific method can be used as a model of understanding Six Sigma.

Scientific Method as a Model for Understanding Six Sigma

As can be seen, scientific method uses everything grounded to determine the best course of action or a possible change in action for a company. Here is a quick example to show how scientific method can be used as a model for understanding Six Sigma.

Supermarket A is losing business and they cannot seem to understand why. They have seen sales drop dramatically in recent years, and the supermarket is in danger of going out of business if things do not change. As a result, the company decides there has been a shift in what customers want, and they go along the hypothesis that customers are not coming to the store because the prices are too high. This then is the hypothesis. To test the hypothesis, they lower the prices in stores in the city to see if the number of sales goes up. They quickly find they do not, and the stores end up losing even more money due to the price drop.

Since they have determined the prices are not why the sales are down, they begin speaking to customers to find out what they want from their store. They quickly learn, by getting this new set of information, that customers want more organic foods available. The supermarket company tests this out by increasing the amount of organic foods in a few of their stores, and they quickly see sales skyrocket. As a result, they proved their original hypothesis wrong, only to create a new one, which they tested to find that it was true. As a result, they were able to increase efficiency and customer satisfaction through the scientific method.

Conclusion

The scientific method was one of the greatest creations in our history. It allowed us to look at the world around us and determine how it works in a logical manner. No longer were there odd conclusions based on a lack of evidence, but hard facts determined through trial and error.

This has helped the process of Six Sigma because it allows companies to look at why something may not be working for a company and how to fix it. This means instead of assuming what the problems may be, companies can now conduct experiments to determine how best to proceed in their actions. It is important companies do not assume the reasons for problems that may be affecting them. Like the supermarket company you looked at in that example, if the company simply guessed it was because of prices and kept to the course of lowering prices, it would be out of business. Yet, its management formed a hypothesis, tested it, and when it failed, they created a new hypothesis based on what they had learned, which turned out to be true.

This is the key to Six Sigma and the importance of the scientific method in finding the right solutions to the problems companies face.

The Six Sigma Manual

Chapter 4
Six Sigma Modeling

"These same experiences make of the sequence of life cycles a generational cycle, irrevocably binding each generation to those that gave it life and to those for whose life it is responsible. Thus, reconciling lifelong generativity and stagnation involves the elder in a review of his or her own years of active responsibility for nurturing the next generations, and also in an integration of earlier-life experiences of caring and of self-concern in relation to previous generations."

-Erik H. Erickson

Introduction

Everything has a life cycle, from the lowest bacteria to the largest galaxy. Over time, everything goes through the process of growth, peak, and decline. Whether it is us, other animals, planets, stars, or the universe — everything grows and shrinks over time.

Six Sigma is much the same as everything else. Six Sigma Modeling refers to the life cycle of Six Sigma divided into its key phases. These phases will be outlined in more detail in the chapter, but quickly they are:

- Project Selection
- Team Creation
- Developing the Charter
- Team Training
- Implement DMAIC
- Project Closeout and Implementation

These are the key phases of Six Sigma and they are how the Six Sigma strategy is created. Done with a phase missing or in the wrong order, the entire Six Sigma strategy of a company is doomed to failure. As a result, it is extremely important you know exactly what the phases are, how they fit together in the cycle, and why they are important to the Six Sigma process.

The Six Phases of Six Sigma

As outlined before, the six phases of the Six Sigma life cycle are Project Selection, Team Creation, Develop the Charter, Team Training, Implement DMAIC, Project Closeout, and Implementation.

Project Selection

When you start on a Six Sigma project, you are working toward the means that will help improvements in the Six Sigma deployment be realized. To achieve these improvements, areas such as quality and cost, customer, and employee needs all have to be addressed. Therefore, Six Sigma projects must be defined and managed clearly to help these goals and improvements be realized.

But how do you go about selecting the proper project for your company? You want it to raise your efficiency so you are not spending upwards of 20 percent of the revenue on quality issues. Therefore, you should select projects that are based on a suitable cost-benefit analysis. How do you come to that conclusion? When you are looking at all the factors related to the project, what is the possibility of success? Knowing the probability of success by assessing the factors will allow the company to see more success at the completion of the project.

There are several criteria to look at when you are determining if there is a probability of success. You want to find out if any of the following will happen, because if they do, the probability of success increases significantly.

- Decreased costs on materials
- Increased sales due to the increase of inventory
- Lower labor costs
- Lower maintenance costs
- Lower time to get the product to the customer
- Increased morale among employees
- Lower use of materials

If any of these things happens, you can bet that the probability of success will increase. If you can show there will be decreased costs on materials, delivery time to customers, and lower labor costs, then you are able to see that this will create greater customer satisfaction, which generates more sales on products that do not cost as much to make.

Your projects must be focused on the right goals; this is the responsibility of any leader. They need to be able to show the group or team why they are implementing this project, why they are spending their time on it, and what rewards they can possibly get out of it at the end through a healthier company.

Most Six Sigma projects will be selected based on two different criteria: either it is good for the customer or the shareholders.

For customer-value projects, which most Six Sigma projects are, the end result needs to have a positive impact on the customers. As a result, you need to be able to link the practices of the company with the perceived benefit and value the customer will put into it. Learning what customers are looking for is primarily something that has to be done directly with the customer. The last chapter addressed the issue of assuming what customers want will only lead to disaster. Companies have to speak with the customers through a variety of methods to determine what will be best for the company based on what the customer wants. Remember the Voice of the Customer? Well, it applies here because the Voice of the Customer has the power to move mountains, and any company that fails to listen or gear most of its projects to provide a positive impact on the customer is doomed to failure.

The other type of project companies initiate in their Six Sigma goal is the Shareholder Value Project. This type of project addresses the efficiency and revenue of the company and also how it affects the shareholders. This is not used as much because most companies need to be accountable to the customer; without customers, there is no business for the shareholders to make money off of.

While these are the two main projects that can be selected by a company, there are other ones that are not used. They include:

- Employee Morale
- Environmental Issues
- Regulatory Concerns

Picking a project is a delicate process of evaluating, aligning, and prioritizing. You have to make sure that your Six Sigma project will solve the right problems and not create any new ones. Look at the evaluation, alignment, and priority that companies need to do when selecting a Six Sigma project.

Chapter 4: Six Sigma Modeling

The evaluation of a project looks at how it will contribute to a specific area of the business. The probability of success and also how it will affect the customers and the shareholders have to be addressed.

The benefits from this evaluation allow companies to see the quantifiable improvements and quantifiable returns of the project. Quantifiable improvements are something like getting a 90 percent gain over the performance in certain key metrics, while quantifiable returns are returns on investments over the course of one year.

The alignment of the project is how it relates to the goals and strategies of the business. The project needs to be evaluated for how the project will help the business needs of the entire company. The project should be categorized in hard dollar value of at least 75 percent; no more than 25 percent of Six Sigma project should be soft-saving projects. The project should be aligned to the overall business to ensure the efforts and contributions of the project and its team members are used properly. The project should have a positive learning value and contribute to the next bit of momentum for the total Six Sigma initiative at the company.

The priority of the project should also be assessed to determine what projects will need the most money, time, and commitment, and also which ones will have the largest potential impact on the organization, either strategically or financially.

Team Creation

To allow a project to be completed properly, in a manner that will allow the company to benefit fully, is one of the main goals of Six Sigma. As a result, team formation is a crucial step in this process. To begin with, a company needs to assess what parts of the company can be deemed as stakeholders in the process. These are the groups that will benefit the most, or lose the most if it fails, in the project for the company. For example, upgrading the financial software of the company to make it more efficient will benefit, and risk, the most for those in accounting.

When a company knows who the stakeholders are, they need to take a representative from each stakeholder group. These need to be individuals who have the backing of management, are ready for change, and are able to work in a team environment. Try and limit the team size to about five to seven members — too many and you risk getting too many cooks in the kitchen and there will be no progress. As with any team atmosphere, there are things that can create an inefficient team, and these are things every manager needs to watch for if they want the project and company's progress to Six Sigma to be successful.

1. If there are no monitor evaluators, teams may not weigh the options of their decisions. This can lead to bad decisions, and bad decisions are bad for the company and its revenue.

2. If there are too many monitor evaluators, it is the same as having too many cooks in the kitchen, too many voices speaking up, and creative innovations are stifled for the status quo.

3. No completer or finishers on a team will have a team with good strategies, but no way to follow through on completion.

On the flip side, there are things that can be done to create an effective team for the project.

1. Have a plant on the team who can lead to more ideas and better strategies.

Chapter 4: Six Sigma Modeling

2. Resource investigators will be able to look at what is available to help turn the team into a productive machine.

3. Shapers are those who have a sense of urgency to get the results out there. These are the people who make high-performance teams.

4. Team workers are the ones who help keep shapers in line and keep conflict to a minimum.

5. A specialist is someone on the team who has the know-how and the understanding of the task at hand.

Naturally, you may be wondering what all these roles are on the team, so here is a quick outline that will allow you to see the roles that make up teams and also their strengths and weaknesses.

TEAM ROLE	CONTRIBUTION	WEAKNESSES
Plant	Creative, thinks outside the box, and can solve problems others cannot.	Does not think about details and communicate well.
Resource Investigator	Extroverted and excited about the project. Can communicate well and knows the opportunities.	Too optimistic and can lose interest quickly.
Coordinator	Mature and confident and has the courage to get over the obstacles.	Delegates personal work to others that could be done themselves.
Shaper	They are dynamic and good under pressure. Like the coordinator, they have the courage to handle obstacles.	Too confrontational with others and can provoke others into arguments.
Monitor Evaluator	Strategic and looks at everything before making a decision.	Does not have the drive of others; can be critical.

TEAM ROLE	CONTRIBUTION	WEAKNESSES
Team Worker	Extremely cooperative and diplomatic with other team members. Listens and does their job.	Not the best in high-pressure situations and can be influenced easily.
Implementer	Reliable and efficient, with an ability to turn actions into results.	Is not always flexible and will resist change.
Finisher	Anxious and painstaking in their work. They deliver on time, while searching out all the results.	Worries too much and is a nit-picker.
Specialist	Self-starting and dedicated to the job. Has the knowledge and the skills vitally needed for the team.	Does not look at the big picture and only contributes on a small portion of the project.

Looking at this, you may think, "Why have any of them?" Well, the truth is that you want to have most of these types on your team because the faults of each person will be negated by the strengths of others, and vice versa.

Develop the Charter

The project charter, or project definition, ensures that all the details of the project are documented, while giving the opportunity to update them on a regular basis as new information comes into the project. The key tasks that should be defined in the charter are:

- The project statement and what the business needs are for doing the project.

- The scope of the project, including the preliminary data that may be at the disposal of the team.

- The deliverables and the useful output of the project.

- The schedule of initial project milestones.

- The project stakeholders and the representatives from each group form a cohesive group or team.

- The date of the kickoff meeting and a meeting schedule.

- An agreement of the project scope and the deliverables.

- The process at its top level (mapped).

- The approval of the project charter from the project sponsor.

These tasks ensure the projects can be controlled and managed. They are the contract between the project sponsor and the team for the project, but the charter can be updated on a regular basis.

Project charters help teams avoid projects that deal with:

- Unimportant issues

- Conflicts with other projects

- Obsolete products or processes

- Poorly defined scopes

- Studying the symptoms of the problems in the company, rather than looking at the root causes

- Poor deliverables

- A lack of management authority or management responsibility

Team Development

Just as important as creating the team is the development of the team. The team needs to be trained in the skills of the project, and they have to develop into a workable dynamic that will help make the project and the team a success.

In team development, there are four main stages: forming, storming, norming, and performing. Examine these a bit further:

1. The forming stage is when all the team members are polite to each other. Ground rules are respected and there is no friction because no one has truly gotten into the problem-solving of the process.

2. In the storming stage, the team has begun to work at the problems they are being presented with. This includes brainstorming together and looking at the available data. Conflicts begin to develop at this stage due to people with opposing views of the direction of the project. Team members quickly begin to establish their roles, which then undermines the authority of the team leader and causes problems with the team's process. At this point, the team leader needs to lay down the ground rules of the project. If the team leader does not, the team may not be able to move forward properly to the next stage.

3. The norming stage is when the team starts to make progress. Everyone reaches a stage of independent thinking, which then allows them to problem-solve properly in the group.

4. The performing stage means that the team is working well, making good progress, and has confidence. They are a highly efficient team at this point.

Implement DMAIC

You will learn about DMAIC in a later section, so here a summary will be presented about what the different letters mean and how they work in the completion of a project.

- Define: This is knowing the goals of the improvement strategy.

- Measure: This is looking at the current system and measuring its success rate.

- Analyze: This is looking at ways to eliminate the gap between the current performance of the system and desired goals.

- Improve: This is improving the system to get it to the Six Sigma level of efficiency.

- Control: This is controlling the new system and ensuring it stays at the Six Sigma level.

Project Closeout and Implementation

At this point, the project has been completed, the team has gone back to their selective groups, and the project is ready to implement itself into the company. If the project has reached this stage, then it has gone through the major steps to getting the job done, and it is now time for everyone to celebrate a job well done and begin working on the next process.

Remember, Six Sigma is not something that is done quickly or easily. It takes a lot of work and a lot of effort in the completion of many projects to move up just six percentage points in efficiency from Three Sigma to Six Sigma.

Conclusion

In this chapter, you learned that Six Sigma is no different from anything else, as it, too, has a life cycle. As a result, it needs to go through the same steps to make the projects within the Six Sigma completion process successful. This means that a lot of work has to go into putting it all together, as you learned here. Through all the steps that relate to completing a project and modeling the life cycle of Six Sigma processes, every one of them has to play a part in its completion. There is no one person who simply takes the helm and decides how everything will go and how they will do it all themselves. Everyone plays a part and everyone has to be heading in the same direction to make it happen. Looking at the teams and how they are formed, it is clear that everyone needs to be working together. If one person does not work with everyone else, it means that the entire project process can fail, and if that fails, it means a serious setback in the process of making the Six Sigma transition for the company a reality.

The top-level sponsors need to have trust in their management teams to be able to put together the right combination of stakeholders from various groups to create a team that will work. They will be spending a lot of time together and they need to be on the same page. Conflicts will happen, but when there is a good mix of people who can all work together for a satisfactory end result, it means the success of the project.

If a company simply throws together those who seem to work the best together into a group, then this does not necessarily mean success. It could result in the individuals not caring about the project; it could be the result of the lack of ideas, but the project may be doomed to failure. There needs to be a healthy mix of liberals and conservatives, antagonists and protagonists, dominant and submissive, extroverted and introverted. If you have too many antagonists on a team, then the team will simply fight amongst each other. If you have too many submissive people on the team, then nothing will get done because no one wants to stand up and make a decision.

When a company is going through the project process and the modeling of Six Sigma projects, it needs to think of the team dynamic as the most important part of the project. Failure to do so is the end of that project's success.

Section Conclusion

"The first rule of any technology used in a business is that automation applied to an efficient operation will magnify the efficiency. The second is that automation applied to an inefficient operation will magnify the inefficiency."

- Bill Gates

"We have a criminal jury system which is superior to any in the world; and its efficiency is only marred by the difficulty of finding twelve men every day who don't know anything and can't read."

- Mark Twain

The world of Six Sigma is not exactly an easy one to understand. It involves taking a significant amount of information into consideration, plotting graphs, creating teams, and delving into serious problem solving.

Throughout this section, you have looked at what makes Six Sigma tick and why it is being considered one of the best ways companies can work toward a common goal of maximized efficiency, customer satisfaction, and revenue streams.

Like so many other revolutionary ideas, this one came about because there was time for a change and someone stood up and said, "I will make that change."

Bill Smith was a lot like the Six Sigma that he helped to create. He pushed himself to engineer new solutions for himself and he put that determination and free thinking into his work. As a result, Six Sigma was born.

Motorola and many other businesses have benefited from Six Sigma. Those businesses amount to a huge portion of the world's economy.

In this section, you learned that Six Sigma is not just an idea, but it is a set series of guidelines that need to be followed to obtain a desired result. It involves understanding complex terminology that does not make total sense. It involves being a student of the scientific method and looking at individuals, their strengths and their weaknesses, and trying to figure out how everyone will work together when they are put in groups.

It is not an easy thing to do but if it was, everyone else would be doing it by now. Instead, a select few companies have shown themselves to be innovators by implementing the Six Sigma practices in their own company, and as you learned from the statistics in the introduction, they were the better for it.

Section 2
Six Sigma Leadership

"In order to be a leader, a man must have followers. And to have followers, a man must have their confidence. Hence, the supreme quality for a leader is unquestionably integrity. Without it, no real success is possible, no matter whether it is on a section gang, a football field, in an army, or in an office. If a man's associates find him guilty of being phony, if they find that he lacks forthright integrity, he will fail. His teachings and actions must square with each other. The first great need, therefore, is integrity and high purpose."

-Dwight D. Eisenhower

What is leadership? It is something that everyone can be born with or is it something you have to craft for yourself? Is it something that someone can teach you? Or can you only teach yourself to be a leader?

Looking at the companies that use Six Sigma, it is easy to see they are leaders in their industry sector. They are the companies that are taking up the initiative and pushing themselves to continually do better and strive for better customer service and efficiency.

In business, it is only the strong that survive, and to be strong, you have to be a leader. This is why these companies that have been outlined in the book have survived, because they are leaders.

This next section is going to reveal what is required, not from the team members who do the work, but from the leaders, who initiate the process and get things going with their ability to delegate, lead by example, and inspire those under them.

This is one of the most important sections because it will allow you to understand just what it takes to be able to lead in a Six Sigma company. You will understand the attitudes and organization structure that is necessary to successfully implement the Six Sigma processes. You will know what is needed by leaders to get the ball rolling and move it all the way to completion.

You will learn about green, black, and master black belts in Six Sigma and how each has a different leadership role to play.

This section will show you what is required of you and it is up to you to decide if you have it in you. Leading a Six Sigma transition for a company is no picnic. It is a lot of hard work and determination and only those who are forward-looking, visionary, and enlightened will be able to make it through without any major complications.

You need to ask yourself, are you ready for Six Sigma?

Chapter 5
Are You Ready for Six Sigma?

"We can never really be prepared for that which is wholly new. We have to adjust ourselves, and every radical adjustment is a crisis in self-esteem: We undergo a test, we have to prove ourselves. It needs inordinate self-confidence to face drastic change without inner trembling."

-Eric Hoffer

Change comes whether you like it or not. When it is time for things to change, then Old Man Time comes along and moves things along. This creates two different types of people: those who handle change and those who do not. In the business world, not changing can be disastrous.

Company A has done business a certain way, and with little competition around them, they have prospered. Although, with the advent of the Internet and globalization, things have begun to change. As a result, more and more competition is moving into the area and Company A is struggling to survive. These other companies offer more to the customer and have done research into what the customer wants. They understand the changing world of the customer and they adjust themselves to meet that. Yet, Company A refuses to change and thinks of these other places as nothing more than fancy bells and whistles. They refuse to change, despite the signs around them, and before long, they have been passed over by companies that knew to change and did.

With Six Sigma, there are those companies that choose to go along with the new revolution and those that do not. No different from Company A, those companies that choose not to go along with the change are in serious danger of being left behind. The Six Sigma companies operated on an efficiency that is nearly 100 percent, and without changing their own ways, other companies are going to suffer as a result. They need to adapt or die, yet few companies ever seem to take the course of action and choose to stick with the status quo.

There is an adage that "Chance favors the prepared mind," and it is true. Chance comes along and it is up to companies to be prepared for it. Chance soon brings change, and those companies that have taken the time to implement Six Sigma, are highly efficient, and can roll with the changing business world are going to be the ones that survive.

Can your company handle the changes that Six Sigma will bring to the company? Can the attitudes and the organizational structure of the team work to make it happen and implement project goals that are not only attainable, but will help the company advance?

If you think the answer may be yes, then move on to learn more about what it takes to be a Six Sigma company.

Attitudes and Organization Structures Necessary for Six Sigma

When your company is in the process of switching over to Six Sigma or is considering doing it because you want to reach a new level of efficiency, it is not as easy as simply stating to everyone, "We are going to be Six Sigma!"

Unfortunately, while Six Sigma can be initiated by one individual at the top of the organization, it takes more than just that person to get everything rolling.

The entire company and every employee must buy into it because only then can the entire company benefit from having Six Sigma.

Why is this? Why does every employee and department need to be working toward and believing in Six Sigma to make it successful? To understand why, you simply have to look at the efficiency rate of Six Sigma. It is an astonishing 3.4 per every one million opportunities. This is an astonishingly high efficiency rate, truly unbelievable. For a company to reach this type of efficiency, every single employee needs to be on board. Look at an example of a company that may not have all its employees on board before going into the Six Sigma world.

A priority delivery company delivers pieces of mail and parcels all over the world. They pride themselves on their speed and efficiency, which has been quite high at times. Recently, they have found their efficiency has dropped and out of every one million parcels delivered, about 3,588 are lost. This is too high for their industry, so they have decided to implement the policies of Six Sigma. As a result, they send out memos to everyone, explaining the new methodology for the company, and they implement projects to move toward Six Sigma. But management keeps wondering why they are unable to get to the high level of efficiency that they want, so they follow packages as they move through the company.

Starting out at the storefront, they see that the staff there has welcomed the Six Sigma message, and packages are catalogued and processed at their starting point in a highly efficient manner that matches Six Sigma specifications. They follow the packages as they move from the storefront to the drivers who transport them to the processing facility. Everything seems fine for the drivers, but when the packages get to the processing facility, the executives see that not all the workers in the processing facilities around the country have latched onto the Six Sigma methodology. Most have lower pay than everyone else and do not see why they should work more efficiently for the company if they will not get paid more for it. Processing times slow down significantly here and packages are lost because of carelessness and disregard for the processes. As a result of this disregard for the Six Sigma methodology, it causes delays and problems further down the production line, which further hurts the Six Sigma efficiency. By the time the company gets the packages through at the end, they track a 2,000 per one million opportunities loss, which is better than before but still much too bad to be considered Six Sigma.

This is an example of the problems with companies who do not go all out with the Six Sigma process. They need to be able to go all in, and they need to have all the departments to go all in, because one employee, or worse yet, one department that does not follow the Six Sigma methodology is a huge danger to the company's efficiency. All it takes is one person or department to be the weak link in the chain, and everything after that point can fall apart.

A total buy-in to the program by everyone is imperative because every single person in the company needs to be going along with the Six Sigma process. The company is an organism, and all the departments are different parts of that body, with the people representing the cells. If there is a bad cell in a part of the body,

Chapter 5: Are You Ready for Six Sigma?

it can spread itself and become a disease. In the company, one bad employee can corrupt those around them, which then turns that department into a liability instead of an asset. Nonetheless, companies cannot just cut away the department, no different than you would not want to cut away your arm. Still, how much harder are things in your life if you do not have an arm that works properly? You can still get things done, but your efficiency will be lower.

Every person, department, and belief in the company needs to be on board with the Six Sigma methodology to achieve success.

In the Introduction, you learned about the difference between Six Sigma and Five Sigma, and it is important to look at it again. This is because the difference between the two is so small that even one person in the company not doing their job at peak efficiency can lower the entire company from a Six to Five Sigma.

| Six | 3.4 | 99.99966 Percent |
| Five | 233 | 99.9767 Percent |

As you can see, the difference between Five Sigma and Six Sigma is only 0.02296 percent. That is astonishingly small for a difference between the two categories, yet it amounts to nearly 230 more defects per one million opportunities. A drop of .02296 percent efficiency results in an amazing 6,752.94 percent increase in defects.

One person not doing their job can cause that many more defects for your company, which lowers revenue and customer satisfaction, and also drops you .02296 percent to a Five Sigma level.

| Four | 6,210 | 99.379 Percent |

Looking at Four Sigma, you see that it is only a 0.62066 percent decrease in efficiency from Six Sigma, but it amounts to just about 6,207 more defects per one million opportunities. That 0.62066 percent decrease amounts to an unbelievable 182,547.1 percent increase in defects. All this, and you have not even left 99 percent efficiency.

This just shows how important it is for a company to stay within the Six Sigma guidelines, and to do that, the company needs to be all in on the Six Sigma process. The company needs to be ready to move forward as a whole to attaining Six Sigma, because if one part of the company is not moving as fast or resists the change, it will slow the entire company down, increase the defects by an astonishing degree, and prevent the company from reaching Six Sigma status.

No company can survive as Six Sigma unless it works as one unit toward one common goal. Failure to do this is a failure to achieve Six Sigma.

Chapter 6
Managers and Six Sigma

"There is an enormous number of managers who have retired on the job."

-Peter Drucker

Introduction

This last chapter addressed the importance of a company ensuring that all of its employees are completely in on the concept of Six Sigma. You found that without everyone going ahead as one, the company is delayed and a drop of less than half of a half percent can put the company in the Five Sigma range and increase defects by over 6,000 percent.

While employees have to do their part to help the company get to where it wants to be on the Six Sigma landscape, it also comes down to managers and those at the top of the company working to help the company reach its Six Sigma goal.

This chapter will address the importance of managers and Six Sigma, and how much they have to do to ensure that the company reaches the rank of Six Sigma. Support from the top for the company is extremely important, and without it, the entire process is doomed for failure.

When employees know that management is supporting them and looking out for them, they increase their own productivity and efficiency, and that moves everyone toward the Six Sigma goal.

Support from the Top

Management needs to support the Six Sigma methodology, and they need to do their part to get the company to the point where it can be classified as Six Sigma. For any Six Sigma program to be successful, it has to be integrated into the business strategy of the company, and active participation by leaders in the company ensure the survival of the program.

As a result, management has several key priorities that it has to address if Six Sigma is going to be successful.

1. They need to define the objectives and the goals of the program. It may be the customers who tell the company what they want from the products, but it is the management and top-level leaders who push the company in that direction. They need to know how the success of the program will be measured as a result.

2. They need to develop the business strategy that will be based on the requirements of the customer. The last point mentioned that customers are the ones who initiate change in a company, but it is up to those at the top to not only push the company in the right direction, but also determine the strategy that will get the company to its goal in the new direction. Managers and leaders need to know everything

Chapter 6: Managers and Six Sigma

about their own company and other companies through the review of markets, operations, customer feedback, and more. They need to know what improvements will have the biggest impact on the company. They need to figure out what the losses will be at the start of the process and what will come through the strategy of the program through the course of its implementation.

3. They need to define the business-level metrics for the employees, customers, and shareholders and their requirements. They need to have measurable standards for easy understanding of the data needed for the success of the program and find promising opportunities for the company to look to.

4. They need to establish the project selection criteria and also the assignment and approval criteria. This is part of the business strategy, and it details exactly how this project will be run and by whom.

5. They need to sell the program to their own organization and the employees inside it. They need to look at the obstacles that may result in departments and determine how to deal with them. They need to build on the strengths of their employees and decrease the weaknesses. Tracking employee progress is a good step toward this goal.

6. They need to choose and train the people who will make up the program team. They need to have the best and the brightest on their top team and make sure everyone works together properly.

7. They need to develop a resource strategy that will keep the best in the company and motivate others to support

and help the program. Through employee incentives and proper leadership, this can be done.

How Six Sigma Benefits Managers

Managers may ask why they should implement the Six Sigma policy. They may feel that 2,000 extra defects is not a big deal and a 0.002 percent change in efficiency is immaterial, but there are several reasons why managers should be on board for the Six Sigma program.

- It creates a larger return on investment for the company by increasing operating margins for the business while increasing the value of the products and services the business provides as perceived by customers.

- The Six Sigma program is focused on the customer and that means happier customers, which translates in higher profits and revenue for the company.

- It gets the company working toward a common goal. Studies have shown that when a group of people are committed toward a goal, they work harder, better, and more efficiently. For companies, this is exactly what they want out of their employees.

Champions

Who are the champions of your company? Well, in terms of Six Sigma programs, they are the mid- to upper-level managers who are responsible for supporting the program and making sure it stays with the overall strategy that top-level leaders have implemented for it.

Chapter 6: Managers and Six Sigma

The champions need to be strong and vocal supporters of the program. They are higher-up management, so they have a lot to say in how the program works for employees, and because of their leadership abilities, their employees listen to them. These are the individuals who put the authority into Six Sigma teams through the development of the project, and also the selection of the project and determining what resources go into it. They are continually involved in the program, and this sends a clear message to the employees under them that they are committed to the success of the program and the company.

So what are the attributes of a good Six Sigma champion?

- They need to display an energy and enthusiasm for the job.

- They need to have the ability to motivate others toward a common goal.

- They need to be able to show how Six Sigma relates to the success of the company and its employees.

- They need to understand the financial and technical aspects of Six Sigma.

- They need to deliver the results, not just solutions, in the Six Sigma program.

Naturally, it is unlikely you will have a champion with all these characteristics, and that means the company needs to implement workshops to help train people to be the champions the company needs to make the Six Sigma program successful. In these workshops, they need to learn a lot of skills, including:

- Understanding and committing to the role as a manager and champion, along with the responsibilities that come with it to make the Six Sigma program successful for the company.

- Defining the selection of projects, how it is done, and how it should align itself with business objectives.

- Selecting the right Six Sigma projects to match the criteria of the business objectives.

Going further, you can look at what else a Six Sigma champion is going to need to do. These responsibilities are varied, but all are important to the success of the Six Sigma program.

- Selecting the black belts and yellow belts by removing barriers in the organization while coaching them, securing the resources they need and reviewing their implementation status.

- Ensuring that all master black belts are dedicated to the Six Sigma program through a decent backlog of projects for them.

- Promoting the best practices of sharing and leveraging solutions and improvements across the boundaries of the entire organization.

Implementation Leaders

In the world of business, by and large, the initiative for change has to come from the top. These are the people who see what is wrong with the company and push the company toward a new direction. These are the implementation leaders, and they are the ones who get the company rolling toward the Six Sigma goals set out.

Normally, the implementation leaders are those who are at top of the company because they have to be the ones that everyone looks to for leadership through the entire Six Sigma process. They are the ones who start the change to Six Sigma; they are the ones who everyone ultimately reports to. From the lowest members of the teams, to the team leaders, to the champions, to the implementation leaders, Six Sigma is something the entire company is a part of, with each person taking on different roles to ensure total success for the Six Sigma program.

Conclusion

This last chapter stressed that the entire Six Sigma program is not specialized for one person. There is no one person who shoulders all the responsibility of the company. Even if it is the CEO who ultimately initiates the entire process, it is up to everyone to get the company there.

There is no one department that can take the company toward Six Sigma; and there is no one person. If you get anything from this book, it is that Six Sigma is a company-wide goal and a company-wide process.

You learned how one person can lower the company just 0.002 percent and put it in Five Sigma, which means a huge increase in defects. You also learned how one person or department that acts as a weak link or dragging anchor can derail the entire process of the company toward its Six Sigma goal.

That all being said, without management on board and pushing everyone toward that goal, and also without the proper motivation, nothing can be achieved. Support for the Six Sigma program has to come from the top. It has to be the managers who not only guide the process that the top-level executives have initiated, but also show the employees why they are working toward this goal.

They have to be the leaders in the trenches, leading their troops to victory. They have to monitor the success of the program and make battlefield decisions to fix problems and keep the Six Sigma program on track.

Whether it is the leaders at the top who are the implementation leaders or if it is the champions who select the teams and show everyone why they are working toward the Six Sigma goal, the support for the program is a top-to-down movement. It is not the employees who go to management in the Six Sigma process and convince them that the program is a good idea. It is the managers who must convince the employees it is a good idea.

In war, if the troops do not want to fight, they simply do not fight. As a result, it is up to leaders and commanders to show the troops why they must fight. They must motivate them and lead them into battle under a rallying cry; the same is true with business. The managers must motivate with the rallying cry of Six Sigma to get the employees on board and moving toward the Six Sigma goal.

In the next chapter, you will look at the people who do the dirty work of the Six Sigma process. These are the people who take on the processes and experiments and also create the solutions the company needs. They are the Six Sigma Teams, and they are made up of a wide assortment of individuals who are classified as green, black, and master black belts.

Chapter 7
The Six Sigma Team

"When you're part of a team, you stand up for your teammates. Your loyalty is to them. You protect them through good and bad, because they'd do the same for you."

-Yogi Berra

When talking about Six Sigma, you are talking about the teamwork, since the process of Six Sigma cannot work without it. You have to be able to work with your team and your team with you. Of course, that does not go as planned, and there will be team members who do not get along and who do not want to work together.

To combat this, the founders of Six Sigma came up with an ingenious solution. They created a series of "experts" in the process who will be able to guide teams, serve as leadership, and help the overall process of decision making. These positions are as follows:

- Master Black Belts
- Black Belts
- Green Belts
- Yellow Belts

As you may be able to see from this, it follows the same methodology of the martial art system, with the more experienced individuals attaining the higher positions of Black Belt and more. Therefore, the more experienced an individual is in your organization, the higher the belt they will have. The origin of the belt system for Six Sigma came from — where else? — Motorola, who in the early 1990s, was assisting Unisys in solving problems with their production of circuit boards for the military. The managers were looking for a way to promote the expertise of each member of the team, when one day after a long period of brainstorming, they came up with the idea of calling the engineers Black Belts. Naturally, the engineers would be the most experienced individuals in the organization, which would mean they would have the highest belt in this new classification system. Legend has it that the Unisys manager exclaimed, "Now that is a name I can sell!"

Here is a quick rundown of the belts' roles before we get more in-depth:

- Master Black Belts – These are the coaches, mentors, trainers, and organizers who were skilled Black Belts and developed training skills to work with and mentor others.

- Black Belts – These are the individuals who are trained and work full-time leading Six Sigma projects. They often coach other Black Belt candidates, Green Belts, and Green Belt candidates.

- Green Belts – These individuals have training, but less intensive and less focused on more advanced methods such as Design of Experiments and only work for part of the time on Six Sigma projects.

Chapter 7: The Six Sigma Team

- Yellow Belts – These people receive focused training - focused on specific tools and approaches that align with their daily jobs and problems that they will work on as part of a team and help Green and Black Belts in a limited capacity.

Here is a good, clear rundown of the Six Sigma roles and how they relate to the organization:

1. Executive Leadership
2. Champions
3. Master Black Belts
4. Black Belts
5. Green Belts
6. Yellow Belts
7. Project Team Members

Master Black Belts

The name of Master Black Belt has a certain mystique to it, and it is no surprise that so many people in the organization want to be considered Master Black Belts. It has an air of supremacy and coolness. One approach of Motorola in spreading the message of Six Sigma was taking the role of the lead person in the projects and terming them as Master Black Belts.

Master Black Belts are hands-on; they are the ones who teach and mentor everyone below them. They are the ones in charge of the project when the champions are not on hand. They will consult others in the organization and project, including Black and Green Belts about project problems, challenges, and issues. These individuals have management skills and have to coordinate the efforts of this project with the rest of the organization. In a small- or medium-sized business, there may only be one or just a handful of Master Black Belts.

When you are choosing who to train for the position of Master Black Belt, you will want to find someone who has a background in business, possibly an advanced degree, and a background in engineering and science.

The main thing for the Master Black Belt is to keep the entire team on track and heading to the right goal. They have to be sure to motivate and train those around them, juggling many people and aspects of the project at once. They are there for advice and they are there to show others how to do things by getting hands-on. A Master Black Belt is not someone who stands back and supervises; they are in there working with everyone and leading the charge on the project.

Under the Master Black Belt will be their "core team" of Black Belts who they are training and coaching through the entire process. While the Black Belts are more numerous, the Master Black Belts play a critical role in the project and the organization by implementing change, cost savings, and improved customer service.

To be a Master Black Belt, you have to have been a Black Belt first. Here is a clearer rundown of what is needed in terms of skills from a Master Black Belt:

- Highly skilled in Six Sigma and can translate that to project success.

- Can identify high-leverage opportunities to apply Six Sigma throughout the company.

- Has at least a bachelor's degree, and has spent three years in the business, technical, or managerial side of the company, including technical application of education and experience as a team leader.

Chapter 7: The Six Sigma Team

- Needs to have an excellent grasp of oral and written communication skills.

The training of the Master Black Belt is quite extensive. They will commonly attend at least 100 to 150 hours of Black Belt training, which amounts to about three or four weeks of training, plus additional training for Master Black Belt that usually amounts to two to three more weeks. Within one year of completing their training, the Black Belt individual must become certified, which involves writing an exam and completing at least two major projects. They will then be assigned to Six Sigma full-time for two years, before they will be evaluated for how they will do as a Master Black Belt.

One of the great things about Master Black Belts is they have the extensive training and experience to ensure that the project goes well for everyone. They will be able to provide skills that others may not have, and they are the ultimate problem-solvers for the project. They are the ones who the Black, Green, and Yellow Belts will go to when they have a question, and they are the immediate contact between the team and the champions and executives. They are the battlefield generals who are in with the troops, feeding the orders from headquarters to them.

Not surprisingly, they are usually among the most respected individuals in the entire organization.

Black Belts

These are the individuals who are highly skilled in Six Sigma and have extensive knowledge and experience with Six Sigma and everything related to the projects they oversee. Their entire job is Six Sigma, and they operate in Six Sigma full-time.

The Six Sigma Manual

...gma Black Belt will implement multiple jobs per year, while they mentor and coach others, specifically Yellow and Green Belts, in the methodology of Six Sigma.

They will lead complex departments and process improvement projects that require a lot of skill on the analytical side and data side. On top of all of that, they also must implement new strategies and tools they learn from their own training and workshops, while discovering opportunities in the company for new Six Sigma projects.

While the Master Black Belt has more experience, the Black Belt is considered the most vital role in Six Sigma. They watch over their colleagues and they make sure everything goes as planned when the Master Black Belt is not there. Since there are so few Master Black Belts, there will be four or five Black Belts working under one master, so they are the eyes and ears of the project.

The Black Belt will get the team started, and they will get the confidence of those working to grow and help create a dynamic work environment that promotes successful results for the project.

A small indication of the skills that a Black Belt must have include:

- Problem solving
- Collecting data
- Analyzing data
- An understanding of the organization
- Leadership
- Coaching
- Administrative

Chapter 7: The Six Sigma Team

Being a Black Belt is not an easy task, where you just watch everyone do what you ask of them. It involves so much more than that.

Being a Black Belt in the organization is considered an honor. For many, at least those who do not want to be Master Black Belts, being a Black Belt provides a number of opportunities. The skills that they learn will allow them to advance in the company and earn bonuses, promotions, and raises as they go forward.

While many use Black Belt experience and training as a springboard for future opportunities outside of Six Sigma in the company, many enjoy the process of working on Six Sigma projects so much that they stay with Six Sigma projects and choose to specialize only in that.

On top of the skills they need to be good at their job, Black Belts also need to be able to have a number of requirements outside of hard experience.

- The Black Belt individual needs to have faith that management has their best interests in mind and they will know the right direction for the Six Sigma project. They need to be optimistic of the success of the project and, in short, need to have a positive attitude that will allow them to succeed in the project and allow their enthusiasm for the project to translate into the rest of the project team, from Green to Yellow Belts.

- Being a Black Belt means you are all right with change, and those who welcome change are risk takers. They need to enjoy the challenge and feel a need to overcome it. They need to think outside the box and be able to take risks to ensure the success of the project, which is what is best for the company.

- A big part of being a Black Belt involves being able to communicate effectively, not only what needs to be done, but what needs to be said to motivate individuals. That means they need to be effective communicators, and they need to be able to communicate ideas. They need to have the skills that go along with being able to listen to what others have to say and translate that into requirements through what they say. This is one of the hardest things to teach someone, and it is one of the most important skills that a Black Belt can have. Simply put, if you cannot communicate, you cannot be a Black Belt.

Training a Black Belt

This is so important that it needs its own section. The training of the Black Belt is integral to the success of a company. If the Black Belt is not trained properly, the project will not succeed. There is no other way to put it. If you are implementing Six Sigma in your organization, put a lot of time and effort into training a Black Belt. Your organization will be the better for it.

Typical training for a Black Belt involves one week each month over the course of four months, and it involves hands-on project implementation, where the Black Belt is assigned training in a project that will allow them to apply the skills they will learn through the project integration.

One of the most important aspects of the training of a Black Belt is completion of a project. If a Black Belt cannot complete a project, then they are not going to be successful as a Black Belt. Therefore, integrating them into a project, under the guidance of a Master Black Belt, will give them the ability to learn how to complete a

Chapter 7: The Six Sigma Team

project, including what things have to be implemented to make it happen.

This means each Black Belt trainee will come to their first week of training with at least one or perhaps several projects prepared. Having several projects will allow management to pick and choose the best one.

Black Belts will need to be trained to be critical and understanding of challenges; they need to know how to prove concepts that have minimum data and process information as well.

Once the training is completed, the Black Belt candidate will need to pass a certification exam; with Motorola University, the exam is included with the course. There are also respected certification exams through the American Society for Quality (ASQ) and the International Quality Federation.

Since Black Belts are considered one of the most important parts of the Six Sigma process, if not the most important, any company thinking of using Six Sigma needs to look at how they train the Black Belt individuals and ensure they are meeting the high expectations.

The Black Belt individuals in your company are going to be the ones who get you to Six Sigma and allow your company to succeed there. If you do not train your Black Belts well and you have only "partially efficient" results, you are going to be a Three Sigma at best.

In terms of experience, this is what you need to be a Black Belt:

- Bachelor's degree

- Three years experience in business, technical, or management

- Must have excellent oral and written communication skills

- Between one hundred and two hundred hours of Black Belt training

After completing all of this, the Black Belt must be assigned to Six Sigma full-time for two years, after which time they will be evaluated again.

The Black Belts in your organization are the captains and majors of your army. While the generals are on the front lines, they are not always there and they may not watch over everything. The captains and majors are the ones who make the battlefield decisions and have the biggest effect on whether something is successful.

Green Belts

Now you come to those directly under the Black Belts. These are the ones who are trained to solve problems in several environments, including transactional and manufacturing. They are the process leaders, owners, and professional staff. They are operational specialists, executives, and managers who have a degree in business and understand the principles of leadership, statistics, and problem solving.

Overall, your Green Belts will make up about 5 to 20 percent of your organization.

In terms of what they do, the Green Belt will implement about two projects per year and will teach local personnel, usually Yellow

Belts, about how to apply Six Sigma policies, while providing one-on-one support. They also need to learn about new policies and tools through training and workshops, and discover new ways that Six Sigma can be implemented in the company.

The big difference between Green Belts and Black Belts is that Green Belts require much less training and come from the core of the company. As well, they still work their regular jobs with the company and are only a part-time Six Sigma team leader or member. Since they are only part-time, many companies will attempt to have a larger portion of their workforce as Green Belts, up to 20 or 30 percent. This is a good strategy because the more people who are more skilled at Six Sigma, the easier the transition will be to get the company to Six Sigma classification.

Green Belts should be selected based on the expertise that may need to be used in future Black Belt projects. During their training, they will learn the basics of the tools that are routinely used by the project team. Black Belts handle most of the problem solving, so the training of a Green Belt is much more diverse and not so specialized. This means that they receive training that glances over the surface of many things, while not digging deep into too much. Since the Green Belt is like the grunt of the project team, they need to know a lot about how the process is done, but not necessarily the minute details of how it works.

Whereas the Black Belt has to put in between 100 and 200 hours to get the training, and the Master Black Belt even more, the Green Belt training lasts only one week, or about 40 hours. The most important thing they will learn in that training is how to function as part of a team. They are the ones who make up the bulk of the team, so they need to be the ones who work together the best.

As with Black Belts, the Green Belts need to pass a simpler certification to be classified as such, with the exam only going over the understanding of the tools, rather than any deep analysis of problem solving or Six Sigma.

Green Belts are like the corporals of the army. They are the ones who do the dirty work and listen to what their superiors to tell them.

Yellow Belts

This term is not always used by organizations, and many simply classify the Yellow Belts as everyone else. Essentially, that is what they are. They are everyone else in the organization, because everyone can apply the Six Sigma methods in their working life. The Yellow Belts do their own jobs, where they implement what the Six Sigma teams have created into their day-to-day work. They are not immersed in the details or training that the Green and Black Belts are.

The Yellow Belts in an organization need to think in a cause-and-effect manner because they are the ones who will be affected by the Six Sigma policy the most. They support the projects of the Black and Green Belts and, if possible, take on a few small ones themselves.

Conclusion

As covered previously, the biggest part of the Six Sigma policy is teamwork. Everyone from the CEO to the mail clerk should be committed to the Six Sigma policy, and they have to be willing and able to implement it.

Going a bit more specialized, you learned in this chapter how the Six Sigma team is comprised of individuals in classifications of belts.

While the most experienced and skilled Master Black Belts are at the top, highly skilled individuals are underneath them. The Master Black Belts need to be experts in Six Sigma, they need to have a large amount of training, and they need to be able to handle detailed problem solving while juggling personnel and projects. It is not unusual for a Master Black Belt to have more than two projects going on at one time.

The Black Belt, on the other hand, is a skilled middle-manager who has between 100 and 200 hours of training under their belt. They are certified and they have worked in project atmospheres before where they had to implement solutions and ideas throughout the company. They are trained in problem solving and communication, and they are individuals who are open to new ideas and methods. They are the agents of change and they are the leaders of the teams who implement the ideas of management, through the Master Black Belt.

Of course, while there are those who lead the teams, there are those who work in the teams. These are the Green Belts, and they are the ones who have training in everything, but nowhere near the specialization of the Black Belts and Master Black Belts. While the Master Black Belt must take years to get where they are, and the Black Belt must take months of training and then gain more experience before they can be Black Belts, everything can be done for the Green Belt in one week. They can learn what they need to and move on from that. They will understand Six Sigma, but only use it on occasion. They will not be full-time Six Sigma personnel, like the Master Black Belt and the Black Belt, but they will be valued members of the team. It is they who work the teams and even suggest new paths to Black Belts. While they lack the experience and skill, they are still a vital portion of the Six Sigma methodology.

The Yellow Belts are the individuals who have their own jobs in the company, and have a basic understanding of Six Sigma. They are the ones who will use the policies from management, designed by Master Black Belts, delegated by Black Belts, and implemented by Green Belts. They are the bulk of the company. While the others have more training and experience, without the rest of the company knowing the processes and putting them into place in their own position, there is no way for Six Sigma to succeed.

The main thing you should get out of all of this is that Six Sigma is a process that needs everyone on board. Everyone needs to understand it, and there is no one person or one group that decides everything for the company. From the master Black Belt to the Yellow Belt, everyone needs to have a basic understanding of Six Sigma and needs to know how to use the policies of Six Sigma in their own company.

In the next chapter, you are going to look at the process of training the teams. You will learn about what is needed, what is taught, and what each individual should get out of the entire training process.

Chapter 8
Team Training

"Individual commitment to a group effort — that is what makes a team work, a company work, a society work, a civilization work."

-Vince Lombardi

Training a team is something that is important in the Six Sigma process. Why? Well, when you train people in Six Sigma, they will do Six Sigma. If you tell them they should do Six Sigma, they will most likely not know what you are talking about and they will have no idea how to implement it themselves. As a result, you need to know how to implement Six Sigma through the training of your employees.

Which now brings us to team training.

Team training can include a wide variety of ideas and members. For example, you could train multiple teams, each made up of similar individuals in this format:

Management Training: Week One

Champion Training: Week Two

Black belt Training: Weeks Three to Fifteen

Green belt Training: Week Sixteen

No matter how you structure it, the main goal of the training is to develop a business strategy that is based on customer requirements and define a business-level metric for customers, employees, and the shareholders while developing a new human resources strategy.

Unlike many other strategies that use a one-size-fits-all mentality, the training with Six Sigma does not. Six Sigma training requires the first step of analyzing your organization. To train properly, you need to know what your organization needs and what it wants. This means you have to look at it under a microscope and figure out what is the best way to train people to improve various aspects of the company.

For example, one company may be highly skilled in customer service, but routinely has problems with its product. So, while the customers get great service, they do not have good products, which means wasted time and no chance of being a Six Sigma company. At the same time, there may be a company with great products but poor customer service. So the customers may not like the company due to the customer service, despite the good products.

As you can see from this example, while one company needs to train in putting out efficient products that the customer will like, the other company has to train in providing excellent customer service that the customer wants. When the training programs are through the whole process of improving to be a Six Sigma company, they will be at the same level, but will have taken two different paths to get there. As a result, the training programs have the same result, but need two different methods to get the company to Six Sigma, and that requires an assessment of the company and its policies.

1. You need to audit the processes of the company and determine how the adding of inputs (supplies) create efficient outputs for your customers. In other words, if you make computer chips, how does the input of the materials needed for the chips create excellent and efficient results for your customers in working chips?

2. You need to assess the knowledge and skills of your employees and see where there are strengths and where there are deficiencies. Is your workforce highly skilled at putting the product together, but seriously lacking in computer skills? Then you need to improve the computer skills to help the company remain viable and efficient. This assessment will help when you are putting the teams together because you want to know who is skilled at what, who needs training in what, and how they will all fit together. Do you want a bunch of computer-savvy individuals together in a group that needs to put together a motor? Or do you want a bunch of mechanics put together in a room to build a computer?

3. Assess the attitudes of the employees in the company. Are they on board for Six Sigma? Do they want training? Their attitude will be a judgment of the wisdom they have on the particular subject. If they are standoffish and they do not want to be a part of something, they may be hiding the fact they know little about it, while the person who is enthusiastic may be eager to show the skills they have. This is not always true, but it is often the case in companies.

Now that you know what to look for in an assessment, you will delve into the training of teams by focusing on the various parts of a team, beginning with the leaders.

Leadership Training

Leadership training should be focused on the vision of realizing a goal. When you envision something, you picture it in your head, and you want your leaders to picture a future goal for the company, already implemented in the organization, and be able to see how it will all turn out, theoretically.

You have to ask yourself how you can create goals, or strategies, without having a vision, and without leaders providing that vision, there is no progress in the company toward its Six Sigma goal.

The leaders will also need to be trained in communication. As the book has revealed, communication is key to being an effective leader. Therefore, training needs to focus on this vital tool of the leadership toolbox. One good thing about leaders is that they already have effective communication skills at their disposal, so you do not need to focus on this aspect of the leadership role as much.

These two skills then translate into one cohesive part. A leader needs to be able to communicate what they want in terms of their vision to those they lead. If they cannot communicate what they want, they will fail in their roles as leaders.

In addition to those skills, a leader needs to be trained in conflict resolution. This is an important one because leaders will have to "put out fires" that arise in a team environment. Conflict resolution also ties in with a vision and communication skills, which means it is important to train leaders in it. This creates a highly effective triangle of skills that aids in keeping projects on track. Leaders communicate visions to followers, while at the same time they use the vision as a way to communicate through conflict resolution to get everyone back on track.

Lastly, leaders need to be trained on ethical principles. They need to be someone that the employees under the leader can trust. If the leader is someone they do not like or respect, they may get the job done, but it will not be to the best of their ability and that will affect the efficiency of the project and the Six Sigma goal. Ensuring that leaders are trained in honesty, integrity, and moral virtues means the company will have a much easier time getting to their vision of being a Six Sigma company.

Black Belt Training

As previously cited, the black belt training is one of the most important parts of the entire process of Six Sigma, and that is why even more black belt training is included in this section. Black belts need 100 to 200 hours of training in a wide variety of disciplines, including problem solving. Since black belts are expected to produce tangible results on projects that will have a big impact on the company, their training is highly important and that means using the DMAIC methodology to train them (which will be covered in the next section).

The amount of training is going to vary, ranging from three to six weeks. For technical tools in Six Sigma, there is six weeks of training, while a three-week training course is used when training in service, transaction-based businesses, or finance. If the black belts are in the manufacturing world, then they will have a four-week training period. In research and development sectors, training is six weeks.

When you are training black belts in the company, you need to understand that above everyone else being trained, they are learning a vast amount of information and they are learning it in a highly compressed format. There are courses resulting in black belts receiving two semesters of information in only a few days. It is highly compressed, stressful, and difficult, so go easy on the black belts who are learning in your company. If they feel they are not doing something they will be appreciated for, they will not do the training.

Green Belt Training

Green belt training has been covered, but, keep in mind that it will take about one week and it will cover items such as statistical analysis, project planning, flowcharting, and more. They will be provided with software that will teach them what they need to know and they learn it independently.

Skills Needed by Both Belts

When you are training belts, they will need to learn many of the same skills. Here is a quick rundown of the skills they will need:

- Coaching – Black belts, and to a lesser extent green belts, need to know how to coach others because this is how the project is motivated and how it moves forward.

- Mentoring – The black belts will be mentors to the green belts, and the green belts will be mentors to lesser experienced green belts and yellow belts. All need to know how to mentor because all will at some point or another have to guide an individual or group to a common goal.

- Negotiation – Black belts and green belts need to be able to negotiate because they have to show others why the Six Sigma process is important to the company and they have to "negotiate" the involvement of the yellow belts into the program.

Once training has been completed, the company will want to know whether the training worked. This means they will analyze the results of how the Six Sigma projects are progressing and they will determine if the program was a success. If projects are not moving along at a proper pace, then there may have been problems with the original training of that group. And things may have to be fine-tuned to ensure this does not happen again. There are three methods that the company can use to determine the success of the program and to ensure the continued success of the team training graduates: evaluation, reinforcement, and refreshers.

Evaluation

The evaluation is what happens after the training of the team and it is what the company uses to learn how the training went and what could be improved to make it a better training process for everyone.

There are four elements to the evaluation process:

- The reaction of the participants: This works in the same principle as customer satisfaction, but you are trying to find out how well the employees like the program and what they would have wanted to change about it.

- The learning of the participants: You will want to know what they learned and if that changed their attitudes about their work and the process by which they work. You want to find out how much they knew before and after the training program to see how much their knowledge of their position in the company and the Six Sigma program improved.

- The behavior of the participants: This will be done by monitoring the employee and finding out if their behavior or productivity improved after taking the training program.

- The results of the program: Look at the areas for employees who were trained and look to see if there was an improvement in the process. If a group of line workers were trained, then you would want to know if the efficiency of that line shift improved at all.

Reinforcement

Human beings forget; it is an unfortunate problem with our minds. Unless there is constant reinforcement, you will forget how to do something because the human brain will not have deemed it necessary.

For example, if you drive a car once when you are 16 and that is the only time you ever drive a car until 40 years later, when you get back in the car, you will not remember how to drive it. However, if you drive every day for 40 years, it will become second nature.

The same is true in work. You need to push the employees to constantly use what they learned and apply it at work. You need to:

- Encourage employees to learn more skills relating to their job.

- Reward them for training accomplishments.

Studies have shown that employees will participate in training willingly if they believe it will further their career goals. Try to tailor training toward that as a result to help get them interested. You do not want to force them to train because they will not enjoy it, and you cannot force them to learn new skills if they do not want to. However, if you encourage them through enticements of promotions and more, you will have a much better chance of them reinforcing what they already know by learning more skills.

Refreshers

This is what you do to help employees remember the knowledge they learn. These are refresher courses, and they tie in with the employees' ability to reinforce what they know with additional skills.

The wonderful thing about refresher courses is that you do not even need to have an instructor; you can just use a CD-ROM or online course to teach the employee and refresh what they already know. Make it a monthly task, and you will have no problem ensuring your employees remember exactly what they learned, which helps them apply it in their working life.

Conclusion

Training teams is something that is vitally important to the success of the Six Sigma process. You need to be able to teach your teams exactly what you want them to know about the company and its goal of Six Sigma.

Some companies will need different training aspects than others. You will not try to train employees who are already highly skilled in one area how to be just as efficient in that same area. You want to look at their weaknesses and focus on that. That means, as a whole, the company will want to ensure it does an assessment to find out exactly how it is going to proceed with the training of teams and what it is going to focus on. This means it will look at the various aspects of the company and determine the best course of training action.

The training of the different teams will vary greatly. While the leaders are focused more on leadership tasks like communication, visions, and conflict resolution, the black belt and green belt teams will be focusing on how to implement what the leader wants and how to turn the vision into reality. They do not need the same skills as the leader, and the skills that they do share will different in complexity between the leader and the black and green belts.

Therefore, it is important that companies know exactly how to train these three different groups to ensure they all work together properly but know exactly what their place is in the organization.

Chapter 8: Team Training

Moving on, the book has addressed training relative to employees and how to keep what they learned in their heads. The main goal is to have employees be as efficient as possible, and the only way to be highly efficient is to make sure they remember what they learned, reinforce what they learned, and, later on, refresh what they learned. You do this by encouraging them to want to learn more about their current roles in the company and equate that with their job goals. If they think that taking the training means they will be the next up for a promotion, they are going to be much more eager to get that training and ensure that they know the training inside and out, well into the future.

Never scale back on the training of your employees. The aspiring ballplayer who does not train cannot go on talent alone, and neither can your company.

Section Conclusion

This past section looked at the issue of leadership in Six Sigma. The truth is that leadership is a big part of Six Sigma, but why? Leadership is essential because the leaders of the company, those in management and executive positions, need to be the ones who not only initiate the Six Sigma program at the company, but also are the ones who begin to motivate the entire workforce and train the entire workforce to begin pulling together to create a Six Sigma program that will work for everyone.

The leaders extend from the CEO down to the regular workers who have trained to become green belts. This is the great thing about Six Sigma. So many working policies at many large companies center on the executives and the shareholders. They are the ones who decide what is going to happen, how everything is going to work, and who is going to benefit. They are the ones who implement the programs, and they are the ones who guide the programs. While this is similar to how Six Sigma works, it is not exactly the same, with some minor differences.

In the type of method implemented by companies not using Six Sigma, they simply think that putting employees in a room and teaching them something will get the results they want. Then, when the results do not come, they begin to wonder what went wrong, and they even go so far as the blame the employees instead of themselves.

This is not how Six Sigma works with leadership. The leaders in Six Sigma are the ones who create the direction the company will go in, and they are the ones who make the final decisions, but there are several levels of leaders going down the company, from the executives who speak to the champions, the champions who talk to the master black belts, the master black belts who talk to the black belts, the black belts who talk to the green belts, and the green belts who talk to the yellow belts.

Through all of this, there is constant communication and there is training that is not focused on the usual "Do this for the company, it does not matter if you like it or not" to the new method of "Do this for the company and not only will it benefit you in your career with what you learn, but it will help the company be more successful. This will make you more successful."

The great thing about leadership in Six Sigma is that it knows exactly how to motivate people and how to get things done through this motivation. The leaders will talk with those below them and motivate them to want the training. Once they get the training, management will then find out what worked and what

Chapter 8: Team Training

did not work in the training, and then they will encourage the employee to learn more over the course of the coming months and years.

Six Sigma is a constant learning process that never stops, but it all begins with the leaders. The leaders of Six Sigma need to be skilled in many areas, and those in the master black belt and black belt positions are not simply managers who also call themselves black belts. These are individuals who have taken the time to learn how to put the principles of Six Sigma into practice, and they are the ones who have had extensive training to get everything right — as much as 200 hours of training to help them learn how to become leaders. They have years of experience, degrees in applicable fields, and are leaders in the company already.

This is not simply a case of just selecting someone or picking the first person you see. It is a long process that goes in-depth to create leaders out of people who had the leadership abilities in them, but just did not know it.

Leaders in Six Sigma need to be able to communicate a vision to those under them. They need to show them what the champions and executives want out of Six Sigma, and they need to make sure that not only does the green belts and lower see the vision, but that they know how to communicate it to others.

On top of all this, the master black belts and black belts also need to be able to motivate others into going for the same goal. Remember how everyone had to be pushing at the same time and one or two people not going in the same direction slows everyone down? Well, the leader in Six Sigma has to be able to take that person, look at them, and motivate them into being productive workers for the common cause of Six Sigma.

Leaders also have to be prepared for the conflicts that will arise in teams. They have to know how to talk to the people in the teams having the conflict and show them that not only is it counterproductive to erupt into a conflict, but it is bad for the team dynamic. They are the ones who put out the fires, they are the ones who motivate the teams, and they are the ones who have the biggest impact on whether the Six Sigma program is successful.

For this reason, companies need to be incredibly careful in their training to ensure that everyone who becomes a leader deserves to be one. Having one worker who is not on board with Six Sigma and wants nothing to do with it can hurt productivity and the Six Sigma program. Having one leader who is not on board and does not believe in the program will derail the entire process and cause massive drops in productivity throughout the section they are leading.

Pay attention to your leaders and know who should and should not be one in your Six Sigma program.

Section 3
Understanding DMAIC

"On the mountains of truth, you can never climb in vain: Either you will reach a point higher up today, or you will be training your powers so that you will be able to climb higher tomorrow."

-Friedrich Nietzsche

Section Introduction

Possibly the most important thing you need to know about Six Sigma comes in the form of DMAIC, which is pronounced as Duh-May-Ick. This process is incredibly important in the Six Sigma process because it is what helps bring a diverse team together. This is what helps them complete a process or model so that they can share their work and get the job done.

The different letters in DMAIC mean Define, Measure, Analyze, Improve, and Control. These all work together to create the DMAIC process. What makes this so important? Why do you need to know it inside out? Why is an entire section dedicated to it?

These questions will be answered as you delve further into each process. In the introduction to this section, you are going to look at each process quickly, to provide you with a better framework to understand the processes.

Define

This is the goals of the improvement process. These are the goals that must be obtained from customers, because to be a Six Sigma company, you need to be able to please the customers and raise customer satisfaction. The goals of the company will be structured in such a way as this:

- Greater customer satisfaction
- Greater customer loyalty
- Higher returns on investments
- Increased market shares

Overall, the goals must be set up in such a way they will increase things through the production department. They must reduce defects as well — an integral part of the Six Sigma process. When you are in this phase, you must obtain the goals from your customers, shareholders, and employees.

Measure

You need to look at the existing system and determine the metrics that will help you get to your goal, which would be found in the Define stage.

Analyze

In this stage, you will look at ways to eliminate any gaps between what the company is currently doing in terms of performance, customer satisfaction, and defects, and just how to get to the goals set by the Define stage. For example, if your company is a Three Sigma company, you need to analyze how you will get from Three Sigma to Six Sigma, the ultimate goal. Using exploratory data and descriptive data, you will have a much better understanding of the data. Statistical tools will also be important here.

Improve

To get to the Six Sigma goal, you need to improve, and the best way to do that is to look at improving the entire system. This stage is all about finding ways to get things done better. To do this, you need to use project management and the other tools at your disposal to start putting the new goals into the company system. To find out if this improvement is validated, you can use statistical methods.

Control

The control stage is where the new system is in place and it is institutionalized by modifying various systems, policies, procedures, budgets, and instructions to make it work for the entire company. If you do not put into control the Six Sigma goals, then the previous four stages were worthless.

To monitor the stability of the new systems, you again use statistical tools.

DMAIC is important in the process of getting everything together in your company. If your company is serious about getting to Six Sigma, it needs to be ready to implement the DMAIC phases and get them into the process of achieving goals as quickly as possible. You want to ensure that your company is going to be a Six Sigma company and not a Four or Five Sigma company.

To do this, the managers, leaders, designers, and implementers in your company need to know DMAIC inside and out. They need to know how it works, how it will come together, and what it will do for the company. If they are in any way lacking in the understanding of the DMAIC process, then the goal of Six Sigma will die away.

It is important to be a Six Sigma company, and to do that, you need DMAIC. However, we do not want to scare you with showing you how much is relying on the understanding of DMAIC. We just want to ensure that you know how important it is. Without a clear understanding of it, you could endanger your chances of Six Sigma. It is not a hard concept to understand, but it is an important one, and that is why an entire section has been devoted to it and what it can do for you and your company in the process of becoming Six Sigma.

Chapter 9
Define

"Never be bullied into silence. Never allow yourself to be made a victim. Accept no one's definition of your life; define yourself."

-Harvey Fierstein

Introduction

In the methodology of DMAIC, which is a core part of the Six Sigma process, the first task that must be completed is Define. What does define mean? How does it fit in with everything that is required for the training of an individual so that they are able to be highly efficient leaders and team members in the Six Sigma process?

Thankfully, everything about Six Sigma has been thought out and tried, and it all fits together in a cohesive shell that results in high productivity and efficiency.

All of this begins with defining the Six Sigma Process and defining the roles an individual will have in this process.

You should take a brief look at what it is to define. When you think of a definition, you think of a dictionary, where you can find out what anything means in a certain language. However, what does that mean when you define something?

To define is to understand. With Six Sigma, you need to define what the problem is that you are working. The problem must be defined in a way that you can measure it, and be able to tell the difference between products or situations that have the problem, and those that don't. You also need to define the problem in terms of its impact on your business.

The Define phase of DMAIC does the same.

The Basics

When you are in the definition stage of the DMAIC, you have already identified several problems that need to be solved in the company, and you are converting those problems into the Six Sigma philosophy.

Defining means you are finding out what something means. In terms of your company, this means finding the problems of the business and creating a clear direction for resolving those problem areas. For example, when you define that gardening means to grow plants, you can then create the direction to find a solution to how to grow plants in the garden.

You have to create a clear direction for solving problem areas and that involves creating a project. Before you can create a project, however, you have to know what the basics of a project are.

First, a project has to have a financial impact to earnings before income tax, net profit before income tax, and a significant strategic value for the company.

Second, the project needs to produce results that exceed the effort it takes to gain that improvement in the company. Remember the Return on Investment we talked about? Well, it applies here because if it is going to take too many hours and too much money for the company to gain this improvement, then it is going to result in the return being less than what the company wants and less than what they put in. That is not good business sense.

Third, the problem cannot be easily solved by traditional methods in any way. The solution also needs to improve on the performance of a particular process by over 70 percent when compared with previous performance levels.

The Problem

When you are looking at the problem that needs to be defined, you will see that it goes through a process. It will become a practical business problem, then a statistical problem, and then a solution. It is important to remember that when you are defining the problem early on in the DMAIC stage that you understand no matter what happens, all problems can be solved. The only variables in solving a problem are how much time and money you want to invest in it. When the problem is one that can turn the company from Three Sigma to Six Sigma, profit and time should not even be a problem.

When you are defining a project in Six Sigma, you are going down deep into it and ripping it apart. You need to be able to look at all the small pieces of the puzzle for the problem and understand them. It is important you understand this stage of the DMAIC because it will have a huge effect on the success of the project.

If you do not understand the problems that face you in the Six Sigma process and projects, then you have no chance of being able to solve them properly. A firm understanding means a firm goal, and firm goals can always be reached.

Who Defines Projects?

The question of who is going to define a project is an important one. In the last section, we looked at the leadership of Six Sigma and we found those who were the ones to lead the way through the process of turning procedures into more efficient mechanisms to help the company achieve the Six Sigma goals. These are the people who will define the project that will solve the problem the company is facing.

The people who define the projects for you are:

- Champions
- Master black belts
- Black belts
- Green belts
- Process leaders
- Managers and process owners

This is not to say that a lower-level employee cannot come to management and suggest something. They are more than welcome to; however, the project needs to be sponsored and defined by someone listed above.

The Mistakes and the Steps

As with anything, mistakes happen. However, mistakes can be a serious blow to the Six Sigma process, and nowhere is this more

Chapter 9: Define

true then when you are attempting to define a problem and you realize you made a mistake a few steps back. Now, everything in front of you is out of whack and you need to redefine the entire project. Redefining the project takes more time and more money, and it hurts the company in achieving the goals it wants for itself.

The most common mistakes in the Definition stage are:

- The scope may be too large for what the company needs. If there are too many outputs that need to be solved, then the problem is going to be a difficult one to fix. You have to keep the scope from getting too large. If it does, you may end up missing the forest for the trees.

- If the problem is too easy, then there is no challenge in solving it and there is no reason to even use the DMAIC to solve it.

- If the solution to the problem is already known, then why would you need to define the problem? You define the problem to set goals that will be the solution to the problem. For example, if customer satisfaction is low with the company, you will set goals to increase the customer satisfaction from 32 percent to 92 percent, and you will begin to define the project to find the ways to make that happen. If you already know that to raise the percentage to 92 percent can be achieved by simply hiring more troubleshooters, then why bother going through the process of defining the problem?

- If the problem is a management issue, then there is no reason to begin using black and green belts to solve it.

In regards to the definition process, there are several steps that need to be followed to make everything successful for the company. The steps to define the project are important and should be followed exactly to ensure that everything goes as planned.

1. Determine what needs to be improved in the company. If sales are down because no one wants to deal with customer service, then you have to determine if you should improve the product so no one calls in with complaints or if you should improve customer service when people do call in. You could improve both and eliminate both problems at once.

2. Identify the processes that contribute to the problem and their locations. If your company suffers from poor customer service, but only in your East Coast outlets, then maybe you need to identify why those are the ones that are bringing the entire company down.

3. Dtermine the baseline performance you want for processes that need to be improved. If it is poor customer service, 32 percent satisfaction rate, on the East Coast, then you need to set a benchmark of 90 or 92 percent for the process improvement goal. This gives you a clear way to get the goal of the project, and everything in the middle is filling in the details. Think of it like this. The Six Sigma problem-solving process is like a story you are writing. You have the beginning that involves a renegade agent selling secrets to a foreign power, and the ending, which is that the man is caught. All you have to do is fill in the plot in the middle.

4. You need to look at how much the project is going to cost and the impact it will have. If your goal is to improve customer service on the East Coast from 32 percent satisfaction to

Chapter 9: Define

92 percent satisfaction, you should understand how much that will cost. If the cost is going to be $1.2 million to train everyone properly, but the Return on Investment will only be $700,000, then the company is losing money and the problem may have to be solved in another way.

5. Writing out the problem statement is important because it shows you understand the problem and it helps others understand the problem.

6. After writing out the problem statement, you need to write out the objective statement. This will help put down a clear line of where you want to go from your current situation to where you eventually want to be.

7. To solve the problem, you need to start the project, and to start the project, you need to be able to have the people you need to solve it. This step is all about getting the right people for the right job. Back in the 1950s, NASA had the problem of losing the space race to the Russians; they set the goal of going to the Moon. That was their problem and their end solution, but they needed the right team of men to get there. This meant not only picking the astronaut, but also the scientists and leaders who would get everyone to that point.

8. After you have completed all of these steps, it is simply a process of going to the champions and leaders and getting approval, and beginning the process.

Understand the Magnitude

When you are in the Define Stage, you need to understand the magnitude of the problem because you will be able to break it apart better to understand and solve it easier.

In the example of poor customer service on the East Coast, you want to take the 32 percent customer satisfaction to 92 percent customer satisfaction, which is an increase of 60 percent. Therefore, you understand how serious the problem is (32 percent satisfaction), and that helps you formulate the goal.

However, if you only knew that the customer service situation on the East Coast was not too good, and you decided that improving everything by 15 percent will fix it, you would still have over half of your customers going away from the customer service situation unhappy. This is because you did not understand the problem completely. The magnitude of the problem was not the assumed 60 to 70 percent, which would make a 15 percent increase nice — it was much worse at 32 percent.

To know the magnitude of the problem, then, what do you need? Obviously, you need data. In the case of customer satisfaction on the East Coast, that involves talking not only with the customers, but the employees as well. You may end up learning that the magnitude of the problem is not because the employees are not doing their job, but because the manager is quite mean to them. They are having their pay lowered because of cut costs in that branch, which causes them to have no motivation to do their job. Now, through understanding the magnitude of the problem, you see what the root cause may be.

Your baseline for the project is your current performance, 32 percent, and your desired performance is the objective, 92 percent. Using the data from the project, you know you have to get 60 percent improvement, you know the seriousness of the problem, and you know where to go from here.

Weigh the Costs

Understanding the magnitude of the problem will give you a clear indication on the costs that are associated with it. The return-on-investment concept was addressed earlier, and this is where that comes into play.

When you are looking at a Six Sigma project, it should produce a financial benefit somehow, since when you have higher efficiency and fewer defects, you will have more revenue coming in from happy customers. You want to have one of the three types of savings open to you in your Six Sigma project, which will help you determine whether the cost is worth the time.

- Hard savings will reduce the expenses for the company and that will bring improvements in finances. When a company has an extra step that can be combined with another step on the production line, that is a way to save costs and, therefore, increase finances. Anyone with a basic understanding in mathematics will be able to tell you that when you lower something like expenses, revenue has to go up to balance everything out.

- Soft savings are a direct result of the Six Sigma project. These are the benefits that come from it but that are not always accountable as a result of the project. They are the rational assessment of the possible benefits through an analysis of the possible outcomes. A good example of this is that if the company improves the customer satisfaction on the East Coast from 32 percent to 92 percent, then the customers will be happier with the product and happier with the service, and that, in turn, will cause them to shop with the company more and that will raise the revenue of the company even more. These savings cannot be traced to the project directly, so they are soft savings.

- Potential savings are like hard savings, but they need something more to be realized completely. In the 1970s and 1980s, car companies saw that they could make vehicles a lot faster and more efficiently if they simply put robots in place of the workers. They would save money on healthcare, paychecks, benefits, pensions, and more. The robots cost a lot, but the Return on Investment was immense within a few years. So, to get these potential savings, the company needed to implement the robot solution, which then created hard savings in the form of lower revenues and higher expenses. Of course, that scenario cost a lot of people their jobs.

As you can see from these three types of savings, the savings your company will achieve come in the form of lowering one or more of the following costs:

- Labor
- Inventory
- Material
- Cost of money
- Scrap
- Equipment
- Space

The Problem Statement

One of the steps in the process of defining a problem was to create a problem statement. As a result, you need to be able to put one together that will allow you to know exactly what the problem is, which then creates a firm set of guidelines on which you can create the solutions to those problems. Remember, when a mathematician has a problem to solve, he or she writes it out so that he or she can use that problem statement to find the right solution.

Overall, the problem statement needs to be concise and it needs to identify what needs to be improved, the level of the problem, the financial benefits, and more. It is a great way to show other people what the problem is and how serious it is. If you go to management and say, "We need to improve customer service on the East Coast because it is not good," they may not approve your project. However, with a problem statement that states just how bad it is in percentages, how much money is lost because of it, and more, you will find the support for your project will come quite a bit easier.

When you are putting together the problem statement, you need to have the following in it:

- A description of the problem in terms of measurements. This means you do not say, "The service is bad;" you say, "The service to our customers is horrible and that has lowered customer satisfaction down to 32 percent, the lowest our company has ever had. This, in turn, is costing us $2.5 million a year in lost potential revenue." This will have a much greater impact when you put the proper measurements in.

- You need to state where the problem is occurring and at what locations. In terms of the East Coast customer satisfaction example, that means you say, "It is occurring on the East Coast, in nine of our call centers, including two in New York, four in New Jersey, one in Richmond, one in Boston, and one in Philadelphia."

- You should state how long the problem has been occurring so they can measure the financial problems over a set period. "The customer satisfaction has dropped from a high of 83 percent in June 2002 to our present level of 32 percent. This constitutes a drop of over 50 percent in X years."

- You need to focus on the magnitude of the problem. It is important, because now you can say, "If this is not fixed, we will lose half of our call centers on the East Coast because people will not buy our product, and, therefore, we won't have as much to troubleshoot."

When you are putting together the problem statement, you should never be too simple, but you should never get bogged down in industry jargon. You want to get a point across with your problem statement because this is the most important part of the definition puzzle. You need to convince the powers that be that you have a good plan here and you want them to take it under consideration as a project that can be used to help push toward Six Sigma.

Project Objective

When you have created your problem statement, you can then start deciding what your objective may be. You want your objective to be clear and concise, and you want to get your point across.

You want your objective statement to improve a metric of a baseline toward a goal in a certain amount of time to cause an impact.

In that statement, you can see that the important points are:

- Metric
- Time
- Impact
- Baseline
- Goal

As a result, you can understand exactly what needs to be said in your objective statement. Look at those words again and use them in our customer satisfaction example.

- Metric = Percentage
- Goal = 92 percent
- Impact = Greater customer satisfaction and revenue.
- Baseline = 32 percent
- Time = Two months

Now, since you know what you are looking for in terms of those variables, you can then word your first objective statement as:

We want our project to improve the percentage of customer satisfaction results from 32 percent to 92 percent within two months to help increase the customer satisfaction and, by extension, our revenue as well.

To make a good objective statement, you want to explain where you are going to the people who will be making the decision on your project. Look at two examples of objective statements, one good and one bad, to see how this can best be done.

Objective Statement One

We want to improve customer satisfaction.

The problem with that one is clear. First, you know that you want to improve customer satisfaction, but you do not know why you want to do that because you do not have a baseline and you do not even know where you want to go with it because you do not have a goal. On top of all that, there is no schedule, the location is not even mentioned, and you do not know why you want to implement this change. The champions could look at these factors and assume that the satisfaction rating sits at 95 percent and you want to improve it to 99 percent.

Objective Statement Two

Through an analysis of our customer satisfaction ratings, you have seen a significant drop in your East Coast call centers. You have found customer satisfaction there is only 32 percent, and you want to improve that to 92 percent within two months, which, in turn, will increase your own revenues because happy customers are customers who will shop with you again.

In this statement, you see that not only was an analysis done and data collected regarding this problem, but also there is a drop in customer service on the East Coast, which currently sits at 32 percent. There — you have your metrics, baseline, and location. You also know you want to improve the percentage to 92 percent within two months to increase revenues. There — you have your goal, time, and benefits. The champions looking at this will be able to see exactly what needs to be done, how it needs to be done, and where they want to be from where they are. This, in turn, means your project will meet with approval much easier.

Launching the Project

When you want to launch the project, you need to get approval for the project. While this is easier than the other steps of creating a problem and objective statement, you should not disregard its importance. The reason the approval of the project happens so early in the entire DMAIC process is because so much research has been done in putting together the first part of the DMAIC, Define, that you will want to get approval right away, rather than waiting to the last moment.

If you do the project and then get approval to implement it, you may end up losing out because they could say no. You want to get the approval on the project in the 'D' phase so that you do not waste your time in the 'MAIC' part of the phase.

Once you have the approval, which should not be a problem in most cases since the champions are the ones who want the project done, then you have to start putting together your team. You need to ensure you get a good mix of the belts in your project, with the black belts leading. The most important thing when picking your team is to make sure everyone's skills even out. You want to make sure one person's strengths will compensate for another person's weaknesses.

Conclusion

The Define stage of the DMAIC process is an important one. It is where you are going to deal with the project at its base level. You are going to be looking at the project and defining not only what the problems are that it will solve, but also how you will solve it and what that solution will entail. You need to ensure that you can create the proper solutions to the project by understanding the scope and magnitude of the problem.

On top of all that, you need to understand the problem enough that you will be able to craft a problem statement and objective statement that can then be used to get approval for the project, which allows you to launch it and begin assembling your team.

If, for whatever reason, you are wrong in your data and you end up with incorrect solutions, you are going to cost the company time and money. If someone notices the problems before you get into the entire project process, you can lose your support and your approval.

As a result, when you are putting together the Define stage of the DMAIC system, you need to do as much analysis as you can to look at the statistics of the baseline. This is important, because only when you know where you are can you know where you are going. Knowing your customer satisfaction rating sits at a horrible 32 percent will be enough to help get the approval of the champions and higher for the project than most anything else you do. If you only tell them you want to get to 92 percent efficiency, they may think the company is at 90, 80, or 70 percent efficiency, and it may not be worth it to raise it that much for those few customers on the East Coast.

The next chapter will address what to do when you get to the measuring stage of DMIC.

Chapter 10
Measure

"Common sense is the measure of the possible; it is composed of experience and prevision; it is calculation applied to life."

-Henri-Frédéric Amiel

Introduction

What do you do when you measure something? You are taking what you know about it and you are extending that knowledge. Looking at a piece of wood, you can say, "It is a piece of wood," but can you say how long it is? You can eyeball it and say, "It is about 4 feet long," but when you are building a house, assuming the length without first measuring things is a good step toward screwing everything up and having your entire house fall down on you.

Your Six Sigma project is a lot like a house, and you have to be able to put it together properly to ensure it stands the test of time. If you fail to measure, either in a house or Six Sigma project, everything can collapse.

Looking at that piece of wood, you say it is about 4 feet, but when you measure it, you find it is 4 feet, 3 inches. Well, now you know the size of the wood exactly and that, in turn, can teach you how much to cut off of it to achieve your goal of having a piece of wood for the window frame that measures exactly 3 feet, 9 inches.

The last chapter explained that developing the statements to address problems and objectives was only the first part of the entire process. In the second step of the Six Sigma DMAIC, you need to measure your performance, which will then allow you to find the factors that influence the behavior of the process as a whole.

This may seem like a relatively small task, but in truth, it is the most time-consuming and difficult portion of the entire DMAIC process, but done right it will save a lot of trouble and it will help the company maximize the improvement process.

In a previous section, the critical-to-X method was addressed, and that is used in the measuring stage here; it is integral.

So, measuring is not always as simple as whipping out a tape measurer, and when you are talking about Six Sigma, it is not easy at all. Do not let that bother you, though, as it can help turn your company from Three Sigma to Six Sigma when you know how to measure and what tools you should use to get the measurements you need.

Understanding Statistics

Statistics are a big part of this stage. The reason statistics are used is because it will allow us to implement the right solutions based on the right data. Statistics themselves are a branch of mathematics that describes performance with a measurement. You deal with statistics every single day of your life. In our

Chapter 10: Measure

current era of high-gas prices, statistics play a big role. Now, ask yourself, how many miles to the gallon does this car get? That, in turn, helps you make a decision on what car you buy. Instead of buying the 14-miles-to-a-gallon SUV, you buy the 37-miles-to-a-gallon compact car instead.

Statistics are a huge part of the scientific process because they allow us to analyze the data and draw conclusions.

Knowing something for a fact is a big part of how Six Sigma works to be successful. It is dependent on the taking of accurate and appropriate measures and statistics. So, to understand how to measure for Six Sigma, take a trip back in high school mathematics with statistics.

Mode

The mode is the value that is used most frequently and is associated with the highest peak in a given distribution. An example of this is if there are ten baseball players on the field at one time. Three of the kids are 12 years in age, two kids are 13, and five of the kids are 14. The mode here would be 14 because it occurs more than any of the other values: 12 (three times), 13 (two times), 14 (five times).

Of course, when you have a lot of variables and the possibility of multiple variables having the same number of instances, the mode does not help much in the knowledge gain of the variations.

Mean or Average

The mean is different from the mode in that it takes the average of all the values to find the value that is the average and has the most chance of occurring. Good examples of this are seen everywhere, from goals-against-average for goalies in hockey, to the Dow Jones in the stock market.

If you have five students, and they all take an English exam, you may get values such as this for their grades: 90, 70, 80, 60, 100. Therefore, what is the mean? Simple, you just calculate this:

90+70+80+60+100=400

$$400/5=80$$

Therefore the average test score was 80 percent.

The mean is a great way to measure performance, but it is not always appropriate. For example, if you have those same scores but you change the 90 to a 35, you get a value of 69 percent. This one value shrunk our average by 11 percent. Whereas before those students that made up this small class averaged honors, now the average is down to a C from a B. All because of one student. Therefore, when you are trying to assess a problem, you may look at the average and think everyone is doing poorly, when it is only one person. Hence the problem.

Median

The median is the value that is in the middle of all the data. It is the point where half the data is above and half the data is below the point on the graph. If you use your previous example, the median test score was 80, whether that one boy got a 90 or a 35.

Chapter 10: Measure

The mean is the easiest and most common of all the types of statistics used for Six Sigma.

Range

When you deal with two means that are of equal value, they may have a bunch of different variables in them but reach the same average. When this happens, you need to deal with the variation. The variation is the range, which is the distribution as defined by the difference between the largest and smallest values.

In terms of test scores, you have two more groups of students:

83 + 84 + 72 + 51 + 94 + 67 = 451

84 + 73 + 52 + 89 + 82 + 71 = 451

Therefore, to find the range, you take the highest value of the entire set (94) and minus it by the smallest value (51), which gives you 43, which is the amount of variation between all the scores there are for those two groups. That means that all the test scores are within 43 percent of each other.

The reason that you went over these items concerning statistics is that you need to have this basic understanding to be able to put together the graphs and formulas that you will need to be able to measure performance in the company. If you go back to our concept of the poor customer satisfaction on the East Coast branches, you can take the data we have for it, overall satisfaction, and call length time, and determine how they chart together by putting in the figures. To make things simple, you will only use ten variables for each.

Call Lengths in Minutes: 17, 32, 49, 25, 40, 19, 42, 39, 22, 43

Overall Satisfaction (1 to 10): 5, 2, 1, 4, 2, 7, 2, 3.5, 4, 1.5

From that data, you see the overall satisfaction is 3.2 out of 10 and that your call length in minutes average is 32.8 minutes.

Chart this on a graph and you get:

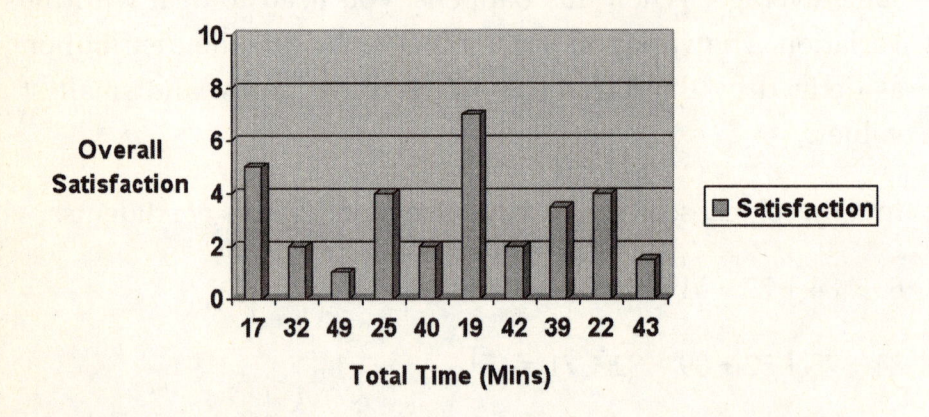

From this, you see a correlation between high call lengths and low scores and low call times and high scores. The highest score (7) has the second lowest call time (19), while the second highest score (5.4) has the lowest call time (17). Therefore, you now know that the length of time in calls is a big cause of the customer satisfaction problems. This could mean a number of things, including that the call center employees do not know the product well enough so they spend too much time on fixing the problem, or that they simply do not help the customer and keep them on the phone.

Measuring everything gives us a much clearer indication of where to go, and it comes from not only knowing how statistics play together, but how they can be improved on for the company.

Having a 3.2 out of 10 rating and 32.8-minute call times provides a good indication of what needs to be improved.

The company can then go deeper into the problem and begin drawing up even larger and more complex graphs to find out which employees are pulling their weight and which employees are not. If there is one employee who is driving up the call times from 20 minutes to 32 minutes, then that may have to be dealt with.

Process Metrics

One thing you will find that continually pops up in Six Sigma methodology is the concept of process metrics. Metrics are simply how something is measured (feet, inches, and percentage). The process metric is essentially the same thing but under a different name.

When dealing with Six Sigma improvement projects, you will find that metrics are affected by three critical factors:

- Critical to Cost

- Critical to Quality

- Critical to Schedule

You are going to go over these issues again to ensure there is a common understanding of how they work to ensure that the measuring stage goes properly, which means the subsequent stages will also work out properly. You will find in Six Sigma that "Do It Right the First Time" is important.

Critical to Quality

Through out the DMAIC stages, you will find that many production processes are evaluated by the yield they achieve or their scrap rate. The yield is the calculation for the production applications, which is found by dividing the amount of the products that finished the process by those that started the process. This will give us our total yield, as in what products did not have defects. This is why it is called the scrap rate on the other end for the products that did not make it to the end process.

For example, if you have a company that makes computer chips, and it pumps out 10,000 chips per day, then you know how many started the process. You also know that 9,987 chips make it through to the final stage. Therefore, your yield is 9,987/10,000, which equals 99.87 percent for our yield and 0.13 percent scrap rate, or 13/10,000 scrap rate. This is good, but not good enough for Six Sigma.

In terms of your continuing customer satisfaction example, this means your yield is 32 out of 100 customers are happy with the service; however, that means 68 out of 100 customers are not happy with the service, which is your scrap rate.

Critical to Cost

Critical to cost is used when you want to track the factors that relate to the cost when you vary away from your target values. To know the costs, you need to look at what they can be caused by, which will include:

- The loss due to scrap and reworks in the system to make up for defects

- Stockpiling of raw material to accommodate poor yields

- Engineering approval times

- Quick deliveries

- Lost orders

When you talk about scrap, you are talking about the defects that do not make it to the end of the process, which is the scrap rate. When something is stockpiled, then it sits waiting to be processed, which means lost time and lost money. A good example of this is making customers wait outside the door during a sale and only allowing them in as groups. The company likes it, but the customers hate it. When there are missing orders or rush deliveries that may not be perfect, then think of the costs-to-the-revenue stream when the customer has to call in because they are angry. The customer will not shop again with the company, and this is a loss of money.

One point that needs to be made is that costs to quality through the critical to cost concept means that things are going to get more expensive for the company as things move through the process.

To fix something in the design phase, it is cheap, but by the time you are in the manufacturing or service delivery phase, it can cost at least ten times as much. By catching these costs before they hit the production line, a company can improve its inflow of money substantially.

Critical to Schedule

When you deal with critical-to-schedule problems, you are most likely going to be dealing with cycle time measurements, which is order processing, delivery time, and downtime.

If there is a problem in quality, this will cause problems with the schedule, so when improvements are looked at for the Critical to Quality metrics, they will also improve the Critical to Schedule metrics. When you look at the customer satisfaction example, seeing how Critical to Quality can affect the Critical to Schedule process is clear. When only two out of ten employees can get something solved in less than 20 minutes and have a customer satisfaction rating over ten that means the company's yield is only two out of ten and the scrap rate is eight out of ten. This means that eight out of ten employees are not able to solve customer problems in 20 minutes or less and that results in customers being on the phone for longer, being on hold for longer, and becoming frustrated. As anyone can tell you, when you have to wait on hold for 40 minutes and then have to talk to someone who is unlikely to help you in under 20, or even 30 minutes for that matter, you have just wasted over an hour of your time, and you are not a happy customer, and you will not be buying from that company anymore.

Conclusion

The measurement phase is a complex phase that you could spend a hundred pages talking about. You simply need to know that the measurement phase is where you are going to take what you defined in the first stage of DMAIC and then turn that into measurements that can be used to determine not only what needs to be fixed, but also how it is going to be fixed.

As you saw with the customer satisfaction example, you knew that your customer was having poor service and he or she was not happy with it. But by taking the time per call (in minutes) and overall satisfaction figures, you were able to get not only the average of the time used for each call, but also determine that the shorter the call, the greater the satisfaction. This action allowed you to determine that to improve customer satisfaction on the end of the call center (improving it with fewer defects could also be argued as a method), you need to offer better training to the employees who work for the company. While this method is not set in stone yet, the measurement of these statistics has allowed you to determine this, but later on you will analyze it to see if you are right.

Measuring something is all about getting it right and getting it exact. You want to make sure that you are able to measure the benefits, the weaknesses, and the potential of the Six Sigma projects so that you can have an easier time in putting together the right process that will provide the right solutions. No different from using a tape measure to get the right measurement on a piece of wood, you want to use the tools and statistics of Six Sigma to ensure you can get the right measurements on our projects. What is the point of finding the average if you do not use the formula right?

Six Sigma is not an easy business concept, and the measurement stage of DMAIC shows that is the case. It is complicated, but it is important, and no different from the Define stage it will lay the framework for what you are about to deal with. You have completed the 'DM' part, but what about the 'AIC' now?

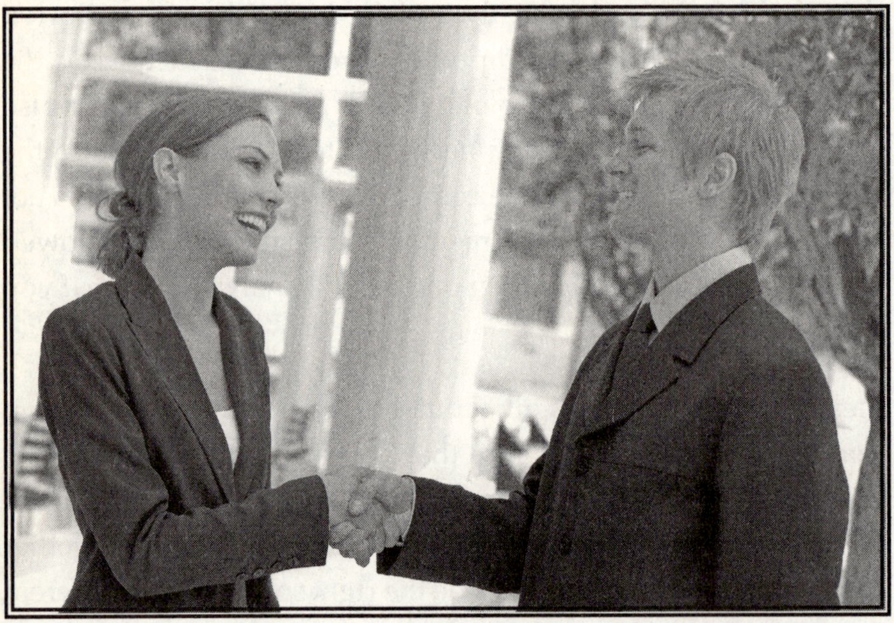

Chapter 11
Analyze

"All are lunatics, but he who can analyze his delusions, is called a philosopher."

-Ambrose Pierce

Introduction

When you analyze something, what do you do? Back in the first chapter of this section, you looked at the definition of gardening as a way to learn what it is. If you still go along those lines, then after you defined gardening in the dictionary as growing plants, you were able to determine that you would grow plants in a garden. However, you also needed to measure what you wanted. You had a baseline of no vegetables and a goal of 100 vegetables of assorted values, but you had to measure how each would work for you. Perhaps more potatoes than beets would work.

After you have applied this knowledge, you need to analyze how you are going to achieve your goals. How are you going to plant the garden to provide maximum yield of 99 good vegetables out of 100 and 1 rotten vegetable? You have to analyze what you want and that will help you get it.

The devil is in the details, as they say, and that is what the Analyze stage is all about. This stage is where you take time to look at the details to help enhance your understanding of the process and the problem. This is where you go through a lot of facts and figures to find the root causes of a problem. In gardening, that root cause may be bad soil, so you increase your yield by providing better fertilizer for the soil.

In terms of your customer satisfaction example, you can analyze data to find the root cause of the customers not being happy with the service because they are not having their problems fixed because the support staff is not properly trained.

A good DMAIC problem solver will be able to look in the Analyze stage and determine what exactly is going to be a cause. Common causes of problems in companies can be any of the following:

- Methods: The procedures that are used to do the work. If the company uses an inferior method to create vehicles with high safety standards, then they are going to lag behind and that could affect customer satisfaction, which, in turn, affects revenue.

- Machines: If the machines a company uses are out of date, they can hurt the process. If the employee is using a computer that routinely crashes, this could be a cause for the longer call times.

- Materials: The facts, forms, and instructions that an employee uses. If the materials that the employees have at their disposal to solve problems are not adequate, they will not be able to solve the problem properly for their customers on the phone.

- Measures: This could be faulty data that is affecting the actions of people. Perhaps in the case of the customer satisfaction problem, the phones are not keeping time properly, so when the employee looks at how long he or she has been on the phone, it is 20 percent shorter than what it is, which makes the employee think he or she is still on track.

- Environment: This can have a big effect on the performance of a particular sector of the company. If the company found that the reason so many people were on hold for so long on the East Coast during the test period was because everyone was stuck in traffic in a snowstorm and unable to make it to work, then that could explain the reason for the problems.

- People: This is an important variable that allows all the elements to combine to produce the results companies want. If a person deals with poor materials, inaccurate measurements, and out-of-date methods and machines, then they are going to suffer.

The DMAIC will narrow the causes into an analyze cycle, which begins by taking experience, measures, and a process review and combining them into a hypothesis. For example:

Our employees' computers routinely shut down while they are on a call, and the training manuals they have are five years out of date. This is what you hypothesize to be the reason for the low customer satisfaction.

This is not the end of the process by any means, and the team will look at more data to either prove that or disprove it. That means the analyze cycle will continue with the hypothesis being proven or disproved, depending on the data that is found.

Naturally, you have to use the right tools to get the job done, and that is what you are going to learn in this chapter.

Value Stream Analysis

The Value Stream Analysis is an important part of Six Sigma, which refers to activities that will contribute value to the product or the service, as determined by the customer.

In the mapping of a process that is going to be a benefit to the customer, there needs to be certain steps that have to be looked at to determine the value of the process.

- There needs to be a step that creates value for the customer.

- There also needs to be a step that does not create any value for the customer, but it is necessary and required by one or more activities. This can include anything from design, order processing, or even production and delivery. Steps like this are called Type 1 Waste.

- There needs to be a step that also creates no customer value, but is a low-hanging fruit problem. This is something that can be eliminated immediately to improve a process. This type of step is called Type 2 Waste.

In Value Stream Analysis, you will deal with Quality Function Deployment that is excellent to compare the process step's contribution in value as it would be defined to the customer. In this, you will ask yourself questions like "Is this something the customer will pay for and want" and "Does this step change the product?"

If you answer no to both of those, then there is no value in the eyes of the customer to the process. However, there are exceptions to this in regards to inspections and reviews, which can include monitoring customer service calls or even a product on the line. These do not change the product at all in any way according to the process, but if they were not used, it would degrade the process, which would be a problem. This makes it a necessary Type 1 form of waste because it does not create value for the customer but it is necessary.

According to Taiichi Ohno of Toyota, there are five types of waste.

1. Errors that require rework, which refers to any operation required to fix or repair the results of another process step

2. Work with no immediate customers that results in work in progress or finished goods inventory

3. Unnecessary process steps

4. Unnecessary movement of personnel or materials

5. Waiting by employees as unfinished work in an upstream process is completed

6. Design of products or processes that do not meet the customer's needs

You may have noticed there were six types there, not five. The sixth type was added by Womack and Jones in 1996.

Process Complexities

You are going to want to decrease cycle times, and one of the best ways to do that is to reduce process or product complexities. In the Analyze stage, you are looking at processes to determine how to make them better, faster, and more efficient with lower defects. If things are less complicated, that is much easier to do.

If you simplify one product or service, then the efforts of employees and the company can be concentrated to be more efficient. The more that has to be done on a product, the more complex it is and the more time it takes the process to go through its cycle. If cycle time is standardized, then the process time is reduced.

Back in the day, the assembly line was the best way for standardization, especially when cars only came in limited colors and models. This meant that there was not someone making four different types of cars in a day. He or she would put together one type of car all day, which allowed him or her to be standardized in the process and more efficient as a result.

When there is too much complexity to a process, the customers can find it frustrating to deal with this and they will begin to not like the process or product and could choose not to do business with the company anymore. A great example of this is calling in for customer support.

Look at an example to see how complexity can make things more difficult for the customer, despite the fact that the company put these measures in place to be more efficient.

> A customer calls into the help line and he or she is asked to enter in his or her account number. The company has

this in place so the employee can have the customer's information up on the screen when he or she answers the call to make things quicker. However, the customer does not have his or her account number, so he or she presses # to move on. Then, the customer is asked what department he or she wants. The company has set up voice recognition, which the company thinks the customers will prefer, but the customer repeats "support" several times, only to find out that the voice recognition sends him or her to "service billing." The customer becomes increasingly agitated and has to go back in the menus to try and get to the right department. Eventually, the customer does get through the voice recognition and into support, but now he or she gets a recording that says, "The most common problem is...to solve this just..." and while the company put that in to help make things quicker for employees who do not have to answer those easy calls, the customer is frustrated because he or she has already been on the phone for a few minutes, and now the customer has to listen to a one-minute recording he or she cannot jump past. Then, he or she gets past the recording and has to navigate through more menus as the system determines what department is best for the problem (press one for a hardware problem, press two for a software problem....).

By the time the customer gets to someone after a wait on hold, he or she is frustrated and angry, and the problem has not even begun to be solved yet.

As you can see, there is far too much complexity to this situation. The customer has to deal with too much complexity even though the company put measures in place to be more efficient. This is a case of the company not finding out what the customers want in service and assuming what they want.

For the customer, things could be made simpler by allowing the customer to call in, enter his or her account number, and be transferred to the employee on the other end. The customer may have a simple problem that could be solved by the message heard during the call, but the employee can easily solve it as well, and the customer will be much happier about the entire situation if the employee, rather than the phone, solves it.

Reducing Non-Value Activities

One of the easiest ways to reduce cycle times is to eliminate or reduce non-value activities. More than 50 percent of the process cycle time is made up of non-value activities. As a result, the first step in the process of reducing or eliminating these activities is to identify the Type 2 Waste. Type 2 Waste is something that provides no value to the customer but can be easily eliminated; hence, the low-hanging fruit analogy.

These can be a multitude of things relating to the process, with the best example being approvals. If an employee has to get approval about something from their superior on a regular basis, it will slow down the production or process, and that will cause problems down the line as a result (Remember, problems early on, however small, snowball into big problems down the road).

If a customer can customize his or her computer during the order, he or she will be happy. However, if the employee who puts together the order has to get approval on all customized computers that deviate from the normal 'base model,' then it will slow the process down. Eliminating the approval process to one approval at the end rather than ten approvals in the middle will speed things up greatly, and it can easily be implemented.

You can also minimize cycle times through a reduction of errors that require rework as well as the reduction of movement that affects physical space in the process. If an employee has to print a status report each day to show how the process is coming (a customer software application, for example), but he or she has to walk all the way down to the printer that is on the other side of the building, it means a lot of wasted time, especially if that employee has to walk down there several times per day.

Other ways to reduce movement and space reduction include:

- Decreasing the distance from the supplier to the customer. If all orders come out of Houston, that works great if you are in Texas. However, if you live in Seattle, you could end up waiting a lot longer for your order. As a result, having distribution centers in key zones (Northeast, East, Southeast....) will lower the distance to travel, which lowers your costs and improves the speed to the customer.

- Less departmentalization will also help greatly in reducing movement and space. An example of this would be someone who is on a phone with a customer taking an order. They need to process the order, but to do that they need to send it to the order-processing individual, who then needs to send it to accounts payable to set up an invoice. This can mean the customer will be on hold for a while or that they will have to wait an extra day or two for their product. By cross-training an employee so that he or she can take the order, process it, and bill the customer, all while he or she is on the phone with the customer, it will improve the process greatly. The employee does not need to be an accountant or order processor, but he or she does need a basic understanding of the processes.

- Reducing overhead costs is another great way to reduce cycle times. If your company only uses one-fourth of the space in a warehouse and the rest is just wasted space that requires employees to walk long distances between what they need to do the job, you can move to a smaller facility to make things quicker and pay less rent on that facility.

Another way to reduce process times through the reduction of non-value activities is level loading. Level loading of common processes will remove all work in process. This will cause the flow to become 'batchless,' which increases flexibility, lowers response time, and increases the percentage of value-added activities. The truth is that batches are not as efficient as people seem to think. The major reason that a process will have waste is because of attempts to drive efficiency further, which you saw in the phone service example. The company put in things to speed up efficiency, but it only lowered it. Companies love to create specialized departments for efficiency. The truth is that specialization is one of the best ways to lower efficiency because there is no standardization. If one department slows down, everything slows down, because no one else can do the job that he or she does without proper cross-training. The customer who calls in to do an order and has to wait as one person enters the order, another processes the order, and another bills the order is a good example. Of course, it should be pointed out that standardization has its problems as well. If that one person is able to do those three jobs (order entering, processing, and billing), it makes things quicker, but if a problem arises, he or she cannot always fix it properly because he or she does not have enough training to understand the processes completely.

Setup time is another problem with processes. It is defined as the time to change from the last item of a previous order to the first good

Chapter 11: Analyze

item of the next order, which includes preparation, replacement, location, and adjustment. When a company puts out four models of one television for customer orders in the morning, but then has to readjust everything for the next 15 orders from other customers who want different accessories, it can slow things down. The televisions cannot be made at the same time, so you have to wait for the first process to finish before starting the second one, and a problem with the first process will slow down all other processes.

With preparation, this involves getting and storing the material or information that is needed for the process. However, ways to reduce this include:

- Convert departments to work cells.

- Store tools, information, and material locally so there is less time to get them.

- Make everything needed instantly accessible.

Replacement is the adding and removing items or tools, and to quicken this process, you need to do the following:

- Simplify the steps needed to replace the tools, information, or materials.

- Commonality of steps for certain product families. If you can make it so all televisions use the same steps, even with different materials, the process will go quicker.

Location tasks are associated with the position and placement of setup, which can include adjusting measurements and putting the supply in the processor.

Ways to reduce this are to simply create a commonality of setups through standardization.

Adjustments refer to ensuring the process settings are correct. If there is a material that requires a different temperature in the furnace, you would have to adjust it when the last process of the other material is done. To speed up this process, do the following:

- Classify each step as internal or external, with internal steps being done when the process is inactive and external steps when the process is operating.

- Reduce time for remaining internal steps.

- Eliminate adjustments.

Analyzing Sources of Variations

During the measuring of the project, a baseline is created from which the project must run. This could be a certain speed (30 boxes filled in ten minutes) or a quality indication (1 defective item for every 999 units), but either way, it is the baseline for which the company makes its benchmark.

However, when there are variations from this baseline, that can create problems, depending on which end of the spectrum it goes.

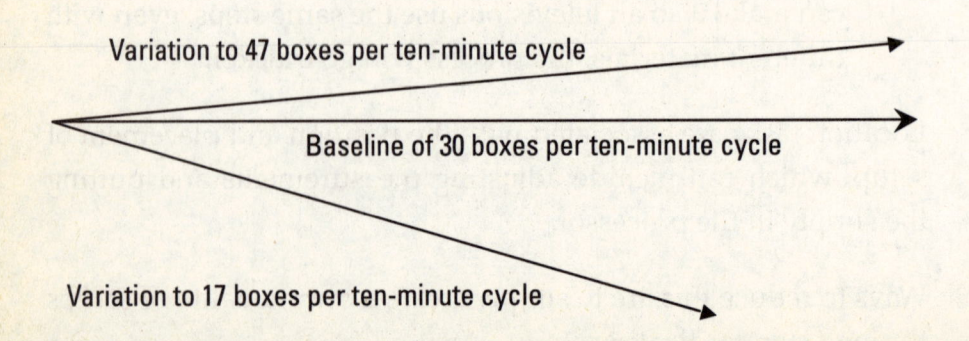

Variation to 47 boxes per ten-minute cycle

Baseline of 30 boxes per ten-minute cycle

Variation to 17 boxes per ten-minute cycle

Chapter 11: Analyze

As can be seen, variations can either increase production or decrease it. Generally, they will decrease it, and the baseline is the best-case scenario for the company during the production process. When you are flipping a coin, there is a 50 percent chance you will get heads. Over the course of ten flips, you can expect to get five heads and five tails. However, when you get seven heads and three tails, this is deemed as a variation away from the baseline.

Previously in the book, you learned about understanding the mean of a process. The mean is average of what you can expect. If, for example, you measure ten different box-making processes and find that the various rates per ten minutes come to 43, 18, 33, 37, 34, 32, 32, 31, 34, 38, your average box-per-ten-minute rate will be 30 boxes per hour. When you go above or below that value (43 boxes per ten minutes, 18 boxes per ten minutes), then you end up getting a variation from your baseline.

Variations are critical in Six Sigma. They are analyzed constantly because variations result in changes from the Six Sigma baseline. Earlier in the book, you learned that the standard baseline for defects in Six Sigma is 3.4 units per one million. Variations away from that can lead a company to go from 3.4 units per one million down to 233 defective units per one million. This variation, which only drops the efficiency by 0.02296 percent, can change a company from Six Sigma to Five Sigma quickly.

A lot of the time that a project team spends working on improving processes comes from knowing exactly where variations are occurring, how much they are occurring, and how to eliminate them to get to the Six Sigma baseline. For Six Sigma project teams and project managers, the size, trends, nature, causes, effects, and the control of variations is an obsession and something that should be taken seriously. If a 0.02296 percent drop in efficiency because of an increase of 230 defective units per million can turn a Six Sigma company into a Five Sigma, just think what a major variation could do.

Why is understanding variation so important, not only for the company, but also for the customer? A good example of this comes from the assembly of computers. In computer assembly, there are several key components that must be put together to ensure the computer works properly. The CPU, motherboard, video card, hard drive, DVD drive, fan, USB ports, and high-speed modem are the key components that are put in the computer. Now, each of these parts comes from different locations within a company or outside of it. If a company is able to put the computer together properly without any variations, there is a good chance the computer is going to work properly. However, if one of the departments has a variation in its baseline for motherboards, then the computer will not work properly, despite everyone else doing the job properly. When a company is dealing with multiple departments coming together to put something like a computer together, variations can be disastrous.

It is important to understand that through processes, there will be variations. However, those variations may be large or small, depending on how efficient the overall process is and how accurate the baseline is. The baseline, as discussed, needs to be the average of a set number of process figures. If you do not do a proper analysis of your baseline, you will end up with an inaccurate baseline, which will then cause problems when you are constantly over or under your baseline because of variations.

Variations also do not just happen. Something needs to cause them. One of Newton's Laws of Motion is that for every action, there is an opposite and equal reaction. This falls along the lines of cause and effect. The cause is what creates the variation; the effect is what happens due to the variation.

In Six Sigma, here are two different types of variations that are measured: special causes of variations and common causes of variations. Some variations will just happen, and there is nothing you can do to eliminate them. When you roll the dice, the average may be hitting seven, but there will be a natural variation away from that from time to time. Nature is full of variations, from the size of animals versus the average, the average weather for a region, and more. Even in our lives there are variations, including how long hockey games go on for over or under the average, how long it takes to get to work, and more. These are all common-cause variations. These can be reduced, but they cannot be eliminated.

For example, if your product is assembled by hand because robots would not work for your particular process, then you are dependent on people, and people get sick. When people are sick, this causes fewer people to be on the production line, which then slows down the entire process, and that creates a common-cause variation. You cannot prevent people from getting sick and taking their sick days, but you can take measures to ensure that when someone is sick, there is not too much of a variation. You could have temporary workers on hand ready to fill the role. You could cross-train people so if someone is sick in one department, they can be replaced by someone from another, noncritical, department. You can also have antibacterial hand washes at each station so people are not contracting germs from anyone else. People will still get sick, but it will be fewer people and less variation.

The second type of variation is special-cause variation. It is called special-cause because it is a special circumstance that creates this variation. If one of your departments suffers a sudden power failure and cannot produce their piece of the computer product, that is a special-cause variation because it does not happen often. The main thing is that you can identify them and do something about the variations. If a department has power failures, then you can easily install special generators and backup power supplies that kick in when the power goes down. This will keep the department running properly while the power is out, allowing them to do their job until it comes back on.

In Six Sigma, knowing the difference between special-cause and common-cause variations is critical. The reason knowing the difference is so important is because they are both different. If you think you can eliminate people getting sick on the production line because you feel it is a special-cause variation, then you are going to spend a lot of time trying to eliminate something that cannot be eliminated (unless you put everyone in germ-free bubbles). The same thing applies to the power failures. If you call this common-cause variations, then you are losing your chance at dealing with an occasional problem of power failures by not eliminating the problem with generators.

In terms of a general policy towards variations, every Six Sigma company should attempt to reduce special-cause variations before ever thinking about reducing common-cause variations. Through the reduction of special-cause variations, a company is eliminating what it knows it can deal with before dealing with the natural variations that arise in our lives.

The goal of the Six Sigma company is to not only control the variation to the best of its ability, but to also understand it and thereby minimize it. A Six Sigma company needs to understand that while it is close to perfection with its policies (3.4 defective units per one million) for processes, it is not perfect and variations will happen.

ANOVA and Nested ANOVA

As discussed in the previous section, variance is a fundamental principle of Six Sigma. Understanding the different types of variance and how to reduce them leads to a company earning Six Sigma status. Nested ANOVA is one way a company that is working on a Six Sigma project analyzes the variances that are currently affecting processes. ANOVA tells how the mean of a response or output is affected by different levels of a factor.

Nested ANOVA can tell much each source of variation contributes to the total variance of the response.

One-way Analysis is an experiment that uses varying levels or values of a single factor that is affecting the overall process. An example of this would be a company that runs an experiment on the strength of a material based on varying levels of a particular synthetic compound to determine the best percentage.

Conclusion

Easily the most important part of the Analyze stage of DMAIC is variations. Why are variations so important? As was discussed in this chapter, they are what can greatly change a company from Six Sigma to lower, like a Five Sigma. These variations can come in two primary forms: common-cause and special-cause, and they can have major consequences on a company's processes.

A great way to describe all of this is the analysis of the weather. The weather is essentially governed by chaos theory, which says that a butterfly flapping its wings in Brazil can create a typhoon in Asia. Why is this? How can the simple flapping of a butterfly create the awesome force of a typhoon? The reason is variations over the course of time. Those little disturbances in the air current begin to multiply like a snowball rolling down the hill until they become so large they cannot be ignored or stopped.

A company has the same problem. By not dealing with variations initially, they can become larger and larger over time until they are serious problems for the company. Six Sigma puts a lot of emphasis on variations as a result.

However, the Analyze stage is not only about variations, it is also about looking at the processes of the company and determining ways to improve the process. Perhaps it is due to too many specialized departments, high overhead, or more. Analyzing these processes means that you have to look at what causes variations and problems in the product process. As you saw in the chapter, they come in the following forms:

- Methods
- Machines
- Materials
- Measures
- People
- Environment

Analyzing is a key stage in DMAIC because it allows a company to look at the problems that were defined and measured previously, and determine how these problems came about and how to solve them. The next chapter, which focuses on the Improve stage, will look at taking what you have defined, measured, and analyzed, and improving the company with it.

Chapter 12
Improve

"An inventor is a man who looks upon the world and is not contented with things as they are. He wants to improve whatever he sees; he wants to benefit the world."

-Alexander Graham Bell

Introduction

It is a natural process to want to improve something. In fact, the whole of human history has been the effort to improve concepts, ideas, facts, and more. Humans wanted to improve their knowledge of the world, so they studied it. Humans wanted to improve the way they communicated over long distances, so they implemented new technologies such as the telegraph, which was improved upon by the telephone, which was improved upon by the cell phone.

Naturally, in Six Sigma, improving on something is the key to higher efficiency. If you define the process and the problem, then you measure them, while finally analyzing them, what good does it do you if you don't improve the process? It does no good, and that is why the improve phase, like any phase of DMAIC, is critical.

The problem with the improve phase is not that people are wary about entering it for fear of screwing up, but that they jump in too quickly. They think they can immediately improve without defining, measuring, or analyzing. What if Alexander Graham Bell had simply jumped into improving the telegraph without defining what it was, measuring it, and then analyzing it? Humanity may have lost the chance at the great invention known as the telephone.

Many Six Sigma teams will actually encounter problems with members trying to jump into improving the process without understanding it first. This is not the Six Sigma approach, and the asking of questions, checking of assumptions, and using the data that has been gathered is critical. Thankfully, before long, many people will realize the importance of these steps and 'jumping without thinking' will be a thing of the past for the teams.

Overall, this will be the portion of the project process where the team and company will develop the modifications that lead to a validated improvement of the system. It is in this phase that new process-operating conditions are created, the benefits of the solution are approved, failure modes are investigated, and process improvement is implemented.

Defining New Operating Procedures

Since you are improving the processes that the company used before, you need to define the new process. It may be a new process flow or a change in the operating conditions, but the outcome of the improve stage is that there is a new definition of the previous operation procedures.

Chapter 12: Improve

Reducing variables, as was seen in the previous chapter, is key in Six Sigma. Reducing those variations come in the improve phase because the process improvements must concentrate on controlling the factors that create the variations. This is the concept of solving the problem before it is created. In the improve phase, the causes of variations as outlined in the Analyze stage will be investigated further to define what is needed for the best performance of the process. This is called optimization.

Optimization involves finding the best combination of factors to create the best response. Currently, the world is suffering with extremely high fuel prices. As a result, many people are learning about optimization with their vehicles. Whereas before they drove without a thought for miles per gallon, they are now thinking of ways to optimize their gas usage through keeping their tires inflated properly, not accelerating too fast, and even coasting. Finding the right optimization means that you have to perform optimization experiments.

Optimization experiments are conducted to teach you the best setting for the input variables you have towards the desired goal you have set. This goal may maximize the value of the output (increasing speed of product assembly) or lower the value of the output (decreasing defects in a product). Optimization experiments will find the best settings for the X's and Y's of your goal.

Running Simulations

Many companies, before ever releasing a product, will run simulations of how the product will work for the customer. Tire companies will run tires on a continuous loop to see how long they will spin before they give out, steel manufacturers will test how much pressure per square inch the steel can take before it gives out, and Six Sigma companies run simulations to see how well the process will improve given the new variables.

Simulations help show teams worst-case scenarios and what-if scenarios, which then allows them to have a better understanding of the process improvement. Simulations will also allow you to determine several things, including:

- Finding analytical solutions

- Analyzing dynamic solutions

- Finding the important components of a system

- Finding how those components interact

- Studying the change effects at lower risk and cost

- Learning from mistakes and successes

The wonderful thing about simulations is they are able to give you the opportunity to look at a given strategy and determine whether it will be successful, without having to take the time, money, and risk that is often associated with trial runs.

Of course, one of the most important things to make sure the simulation runs properly is to put in correct data. A simulation is only as good as the data in it, and if you have the wrong data, you may get excellent results on an actually bad process idea, or you may get poor results on a process that could actually improve the company.

Chapter 12: Improve

The following has to be configured for the simulation in order to ensure it runs properly. Most of this can come from your process maps that you have created during previous stages.

- Number of Processes – This is where you determine how many times the process will run through the simulator. If you run three processes, then the statistics you receive will most likely be inaccurate because there has not been enough processes run to obtain high-quality results.

- Randomization – Many Six Sigma simulators permit random inputs, which mimic the variables that occur in real life. However, to make it effective, you need to have a clear understanding of the process-input variables.

- Patterns – Predictable patterns of variation may occur due to the month-end effects, time zones, distribution, and more.

- Data Storage – What is the data that will be stored in the simulation that is collected over the elapsed time?

- Interactivity – Depending on the simulation, you may be able to interact with it as it is running. If this is allowed, you can influence the behavior by entering in different variables.

Depending on the variables, research, and data, simulation results can vary, and they will either make your day or ruin it. Often, you will not get the outcome you expect and you will have to run more simulations to see if those 'surprises' are common to the new process or just unknown variables in the simulation. Simulations will also create some basic reports, which allow you to analyze the data and determine if future simulations are needed. These reports are:

- Cost – This will show the cost of resources, transactions, and activities.

- Queues – This will report on bottlenecks of transactions in the queue.

- Resources – This will display the resource utilization, activities, time, and cost.

- Time – This will show the overall transaction times.

Finding the Benefits of the Solution

Running simulations will help you see various solutions that could help the process in the company, but it will not be uncommon for you to actually have multiple solutions on your hands. You will have to choose the best solution for the company.

The best way to determine the benefits of the solution is to use financial analysis tools, since Six Sigma is about increasing efficiency to increase revenue. To do this, you need to ensure variable costs are differentiated from fixed costs. The fixed costs are the costs that will remain constant no matter the volume, which can include units produced; while variable costs change, depending on volume and can include shipping and labor costs.

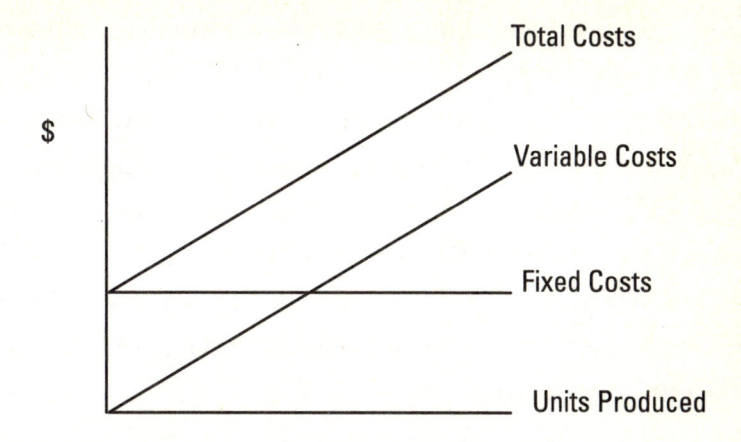

If you know the fixed and variable costs, as well as the benefits, then you can do an EBIT calculation to find the potential profit of each solution.

The calculation is as follows:

EBIT = Volume * (price per unit – variable cost per unit) – fixed cost

You can also use the Net Present Value to calculate the current benefit of a project for each time period over the course of the total time period. The Internal Rate of Return is the interest gained by the project if the NPV of the cash flow is invested in a certain period. Using the Internal Rate of Return allows you to compare projects, with those with higher Internal Rate of Returns yielding a better return.

Conclusion

Improving something is always difficult. There is the belief that you should dive right into improving something without thinking about the data beforehand. However, with Six Sigma, improvement needs data, and data comes from defining, analyzing, and measuring the process to find the best ways to improve it. If you do not take into consideration the things that need to be improved, including all the variables, you will not properly improve it. Since Six Sigma has such a high benchmark for efficiency, then it is imperative that you are able to have the proper data and variables from earlier phases of DMAIC to ensure everything is correct.

What is the point in going over a simulation if all the data is wrong? What is the point of analyzing the potential financial benefit if the variables are wrong? Improving on something is heavily dependent on the data you have on hand.

With the DMAIC process, you know what you are getting is the best data, and that means you will get the best results to choose from.

This is what sets Six Sigma apart.

Chapter 13
Control

"The most difficult thing is the decision to act; the rest is merely tenacity. The fears are paper tigers. You can do anything you decide to do. You can act to change and control your life; and the procedure, the process, is its own reward."

-Robyn Davidson

Introduction

You have worked hard to create a Six Sigma process that will work for the company. You have defined what needed to be done, measured it, and analyzed it, even improved and implemented it, but what do you do when you have to make sure that the company follows the new process? The process is only as good as the people who use it, and if they are not on board, the process is doomed to fail.

Several times in this book, it has been said that everyone needs to be a part of Six Sigma. From the mail clerk to the CEO, the entire company needs to be on board with the Six Sigma process.

Therefore, the control stage is all about ensuring everyone in the company stays on the same track, and it does this with the following:

- Developing a monitoring process to track changes that have been implemented.

- Creating a response plan for problems.

- Focusing management on a few critical measures of the outcomes of the project.

- Selling the project to employees through presentations.

- Handing project responsibilities over to those who handle daily work.

- Ensuring management is in full support.

All of these fall on the mantle of the management members of the project teams, including green belts and black belts.

In this chapter, you will learn about the measures that companies use to ensure the Six Sigma process will be followed properly by everyone and the company will not revert to its previous methods, which is a sure sign of Six Sigma failure.

It could be said that of all the DMAIC stages, the control stage is the most important. Why? Well, simply put, if you create grand process improvements that will make the company a Six Sigma company. It will all be for nothing if your company cannot control the processes and have everyone in the company using the processes as they should.

Monitoring Processes

It is important to keep the process from deviating from its new and improved state. You cannot have the project fall to previous performance levels, because then you will simply be back at square one. There are two main ways to keep this from happening:

- Prevent and reduce errors.

- Detect errors before the customer receives them.

Preventing errors before they occur is important, but can be costly; therefore, many companies will focus on reducing errors. There are three ways to maintain and monitor processes in a company:

1. Statistical Process Control

2. Engineering Process Control

3. Operational Procedures

Statistical Process Control refers to the statistical tools that can detect the instability of a process. This is used to monitor input and output to help project teams to find the instability. If a process begins to dip below a certain benchmark, then the company can be alerted to the fact that the Statistical Process Control has detected an instability with the process, which could lead to further problems. A production line that falls to 29 units per hour from 35 units per hour over four consecutive days could end up becoming unstable.

Engineering Process Control is used on automated devices that will respond to a process variation by adjusting input variables. A good example of this is when a machine in the factory must operate in a room that is 76 degrees F to 90 degrees F for peak efficiency. If the factory increases in temperature to 92 degrees F, then the cooling system initiates to help keep the factory, and the machine, at optimal level.

That all being said, the most important way to handle maintaining and monitoring processes is with operational procedures.

Operational Procedures

The other two process control mechanisms were dependent on variables that have been entered into a system to alert management and project teams when processes fell too far outside of their set guidelines. As for operational procedures, they control the output using guidelines for the human side of the company to follow.

An example of this is that if the temperature of the factory gets to 92 degrees F, rather than having an automated cooling system kick in, a worker would go and turn it on after seeing the temperature rise above the guidelines specified in the operation procedure manual.

Everyone has dealt with standard operating procedures their entire lives. When you buy a product — a breadmaker, for example — it gives you set operational procedures to show you exactly how to use it in the most efficient manner. These are often called instructions, and they must be followed to keep you from getting a doughy mush.

Operational procedures in a company work on the same principle. If you hire a new employee, they are given an employee handbook that shows them exactly how to do their job, use the equipment, and work at the peak efficiency to maintain the efficiency of the process that the Six Sigma teams have implemented. With current employees, new operational procedure guides are also created and given to them to help them learn about the new way of doing things. As well, there is training and mentoring of the employees to show them exactly how to do their jobs under the new Six Sigma umbrella. All of this is done to give the employees control over their jobs, rather than to automation.

That all being said, humans are fallible and they do make mistakes. When they do, that can cause problems for the Six Sigma process. What do you do if the employee forgets to turn on the cooling system and the machine temperature rises to 104 degrees F? You have instructed the employee to lower the temperature when it goes above 90 degrees F, but the procedure is only as good as the person who uses it.

If you are able to teach the employees properly through the process of Six Sigma, this should not be a problem. Knowing how to do this comes from knowing how to teach employees.

Instead of giving an employee a 300-page operational procedure manual that covers everything in the company, only give them a small one that covers their section and their job. Use pictures to show what can and cannot be done, and you will find that many employees follow it without a question.

Training

Training is crucial for getting everyone on the same page with Six Sigma. The training that the employees receive also needs to be done properly or else it will be ineffective for the employees who receive it. As a result, training should include the following groups in the company:

- Operational Personnel

- Process Owners

- Stakeholders

To make sure that the training will be effective in its goal of teaching people how to work under the Six Sigma process, it needs to target the skill set of the audience and include the mean knowledge of what everyone in the group has. This means that if you have 30 people in a group and 24 are beginners with the machines used, you would not teach complex ideas with the machine that only six people will understand. Therefore, you have to appeal to the 24 beginners and lower the 'knowledge level' accordingly. That being said, you don't want to keep the knowledge level too low; otherwise, the 24 beginner employees will not acquire a new skill set that they can use. Look at this chart to understand the best method:

NUMBER OF EMPLOYEES	YEARS OF EXPERIENCE WITH MACHINE
Three (Professional)	Nine Years
One (Expert)	Four Years
Two (Intermediate)	Three Years
Seventeen (Beginners)	One Year
Seven (Beginners)	Six Months

Therefore, in this chart, you can see there are six employees with over three years of experience and 24 employees with one year or less. Using the mean calculation, we find:

$$(7 * .5) + (17 * 1) + (2 * 3) + (1 * 4) + (3 * 9)$$
$$3.5 + 17 + 6 + 4 + 27 = 57.5$$

Average Years of Experience = 1.9 Years

So, for training, you would want to have the average skill level to be about two years. This means that those with half a year experience will have a lot of catching up to do, those with one year and three years experience should be okay, and only four people will find the class to be below their knowledge level.

The Importance of Control Plans

As a leader in the company that is implementing Six Sigma, you need to be aware of how to deal with deviations from the process through the use of control plans. This will allow you to control processes through the detection and prevention strategies of Six Sigma and keep the company on the right track. A control plan should have the following:

- Specification of whether the characteristic of the process is good or bad.

- How the characteristic will be measured.

- How many measurements are required at each point in time.

- How often the measurements should be taken.

- How the measurements are evaluated.

- How to respond to alarms in the control plan.

To understand this better, you should look at the example of the factory and machine in need of cooling.

The company operates the machine that sorts through a variety of parts to send them to the proper departments at a speed of 3,200 parts per minute. The machine needs to operate at a temperature of 76 degrees F to 90 degrees F. If it goes above 90 degrees F, the lubricants and wiring of the machine begin to degrade, causing the machine's efficiency to drop to 3,000 parts per minute, and a further 50 parts per minute for each degree above 100 degrees F. When the temperature hits 92 degrees F, an alarm sounds; when the temperature hits 100 degrees F, another alarm sounds. When the machine hits 110 degrees F, it shuts down due to overheating, causing a large delay in the entire process.

This process can now be turned into a chart that will allow you to see exactly how the process is controlled through the control plan.

Charac-teristic	Specific-ation	Meas-urement Type	Sample Size	Sample Freq.	Analytic Tool	Reaction Rules
Automatic Sorter	76 F to 90 F	Fahren-heit	1	Constant	Alarm	Turn on cooling system

This chart shows that the automatic sorter must operate between 76 degrees F and 90 degrees F. The measurement that is used is Fahrenheit, and there is only one measurement needed, and that is the temperature since it is the variable that affects all others.

There is a constant monitoring of the temperature, and when it gets over 90 degrees F, an alarm sounds. This then results in an employee turning on the cooling system and returning the automatic sorter to its peak operating temperature.

Section Conclusion

Six Sigma is DMAIC. When you look at how Six Sigma operates, the concept of define, measure, analyze, improve, and control is how it has proven to be so incredibly successful. This means that you will spend a lot of your time working through projects using this methodology because it will give you the best chance at success.

In this book, you have seen that you need to be able to define the problem and the process in order to begin the next phase. Once you are able to measure the project, you can start to ascertain if there is room for improvement anywhere. Once you have that, you begin analyzing your data and determining what will work best to improve on the process.

Improving the process is the next level, and this is where you are putting in the changes, running simulations, and finding out what will work and what will not work given the data that you have found in the previous three stages.

Finally, after you and the project teams have gone through all those hoops, looked at everything, received the proper approval from the champions and management, then you are ready to put in the controls that will help keep the company on track with Six Sigma.

DMAIC is important, and few projects can work without it. When your company needs to improve on something, it needs to follow these steps to turn the company in a Six Sigma company. With efficiency so important and the margin for error so incredibly small, there is no way you can skip steps or jump right into improving the process.

No one said that improving a company and turning it into a Six Sigma company was easy. It is hard work, and you have to spend a lot of your time measuring and analyzing, before you ever even get to think about improving. When you do reach the stage of improving and you are putting in the controls to ensure the improvements are used, then the entire DMAIC process will be worth it, and the company will be ready to call itself a Six Sigma company.

Section 4
Understanding DMADV

"We live at a time when man believes himself fabulously capable of creation, but he does not know what to create."

-José Ortega y Gasset

Section Introduction

There are many different models that are used in Six Sigma, and while DMAIC is the most common, there is also DMADV, which is quite similar. Define, Measure, and Analyze are all parts of DMADV, but the two different stages of the process are Design and Verify versus Improve and Control in DMAIC.

The question can then be asked why there needs to be more than one style for how things are done, but DMADV serves a useful purpose.

All through the DMAIC section, you dealt with the concept of improving a process, but what do you do when there is no process to improve?

This is where DMADV comes into play. After the Define stage, which is generally exactly like the Define stage of DMAIC, the project team needs to ask itself the question of whether a process exists, and if it doesn't, rather than measuring the existing procedure, you will develop measurement criteria with the team.

That is the amazing thing about Six Sigma. It takes every single thing into account. Rather than simply assuming that you are going to already have processes in place that you want to improve, it looks at the possibility of you not having a process in place.

If a company manufactures cars, and it wants to improve its production line efficiency so there are only 3.4 defective cars per one million shipped, then it would implement Six Sigma using the DMAIC stages. The process of making cars is already there, the problems are already there, and the company simply has to

Section 4: Understanding DMADV

assess how it is going to improve on the processes for building cars that they have had for decades.

Recently, a wrench was thrown into the works of that, and it comes in the form of high gas prices. Now, people suddenly want cars that have excellent fuel efficiency, and if the company manufactured only cars that did not have good gas efficiency, then they have to start looking at new ways to do business or be left behind. Therefore, they decide to change the production line to building hybrid vehicles. As a result, a new process needs to be developed for building hybrid engines. In this case, since the company has not had this process before and wants to maintain peak Six Sigma efficiency, they need to use the DMADV policy.

As stated, the processes of DMADV are:

- Define – Defining the goals of the design activity, as in what is being defined and why.

- Measure – Determine the metrics that are critical to the process and turn the customer requirements into the goals of the project.

- Analyze – Find the options available to meet the goals of the project.

- Design – Create the new product or process using simulations, prototypes, trial runs, and more to validate if the process or product will meet the goals of the project.

- Verify – Look at the effectiveness of this process or product in the real world.

When you are dealing with DMADV, you will hear the word DFSS come up a lot. This is the Design for Six Sigma, and it is a systematic methodology utilizing tools, training, and measurements to create products and processes that meet the expectations of the customer. DMADV is the framework of DFSS.

Before moving into the Define stage, which will be outlined in the first chapter of this section, it is important to look quickly at the preliminary steps of DMADV.

- Clarify the vision of the project through a meeting with business leaders in the company. This should be done by the black and green belts and the business leader or champion.

- Document the need of the business and the problem it faces. It also should be done by the black and green belts with the business leader.

- Identify who owns this process and the sponsor. Again, black and green belts will meet with the business leader to discuss this.

- Determine what skills are going to be needed by the members of the team. The business leader should meet with the black and green belts for this.

- Selection of the team by the black belts and the sponsor.

- Train the team in the Six Sigma program. This would be done by the black belts.

Section 4: Understanding DMADV

- Approve the project charter, which is done by the sponsor of the project.

As can be seen, many of the things that have to be done with DMAIC also have to be done with DMADV, and, in some cases, more so.

In DMAIC, approval is rather easy to get for the improvement of a process because you already have the process in place and are just increasing the efficiency. When you go to management and tell them you want to implement a new style of constructing everything on the car assembly line, if they think it will make money, it will be easier.

If you tell them you want to create an entire department that will cost a great deal of money but make the company viable in the future, you are going to have a much harder sell.

When you do sell management on the idea, then you begin the first phase of the process: Design.

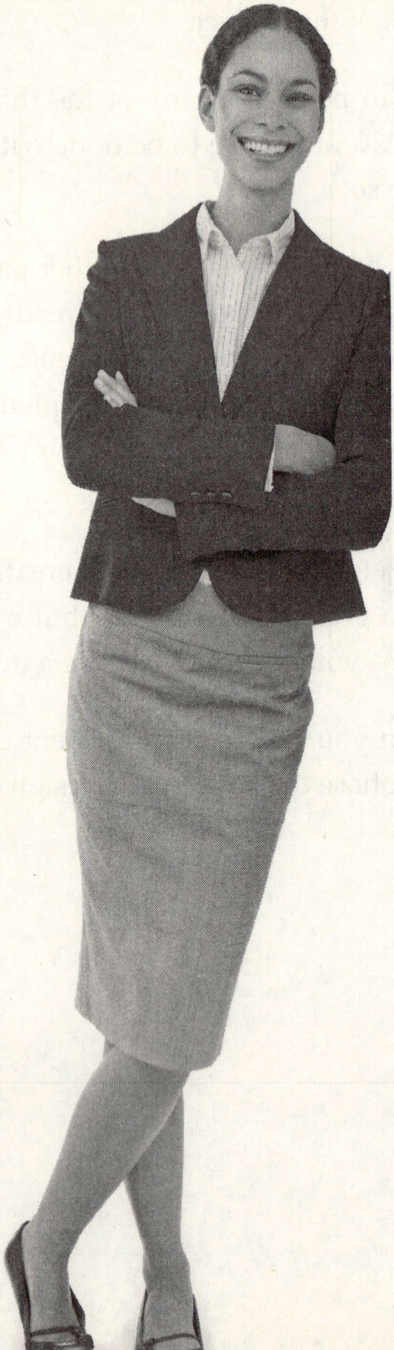

Chapter 14
Define and Measure

"The first responsibility of a leader is to define reality. The last is to say thank you. In between, the leader is a servant."

-Max De Pree, "Leadership Is an Art"

In a previous chapter, you saw how the Define stage worked for DMAIC, and for DMADV, it works in a similar way. Overall, the main things that have to be determined in this stage is a list of Critical to Quality items and the delighters that are Critical to Quality items that the customer may not be aware of. While the Critical to Quality item may be excellent customer service, the delighters could be a system that tracks when a customer calls in and if their problem is justified, they get a discount on their cable bill.

As well, the measurement stage is nearly identical to what you have in the DMAIC, so they will both be covered in a single chapter here before moving on to the Analyze Stage.

The following tasks for the define and measurement stage are outlined as follows:

- Identify Critical to Quality items. This is done by the black belts and process owner.

- Create the metrics to operate the Critical to Quality items. This is done by the black belts and the process owner.

- Establish the measurement systems and validate them. This is done only by the black belts.

- Sponsor the define and measurement stage review. This is only done by the project sponsor.

To handle the identifying of Critical to Quality items, which is the primary point of the Define Stage for DMADV, you use the same techniques as you would in the DMAIC stage.

This means that you want to find out what the customer wants, because the Critical to Quality items affect them chiefly, which then affects your bottom line. A happy customer is a customer who purchases more; an unhappy customer is one who tells others to stay away.

The methods to find out what makes the customers happy are to talk to them, especially through customer satisfaction surveys. This is a great way to find out what the customer liked or did not like about the product, and it gives you the ability to improve on what you have based on their suggestions. You can also use Internet chat rooms where a customer may vent about something, or even in published reviews in magazines. This can be a great way to see how professionals view your product or service and that will allow you to improve it. Even complaints and letters to the company are great ways to find out what Critical to Quality items exist.

Chapter 14: Define and Measure

For example, if you have a microwave oven on the market, and you want to find out what customers want out of the next-generation oven, you would look at reviews, such as the following:

"While Micro Inc.'s microwave works quite well when you are heating up last night's dinner, you don't know exactly how long you should have the food in there and you have to guess. So, your food is burned or cold, or both in various spots. A good feature of this microwave would be to put in quick access buttons that will microwave the food or beverage without the customer having to figure out how long to run the microwave for."

Micro Inc. will now be able to see that to improve on the product and make the customer happier, they can install features that allow for 'one-button' microwaving. By reading the review, the company was able to improve on its product and make customers happier. However, with DMADV, you will be adding completely new processes and products, so that might entail making a microwave that runs through solar power or batteries to cash in on the growing environmental movement.

Delighters are the other thing you need to look at when you are working with DMADV. They are called this because you are not just meeting customer satisfaction requirements, you are delighting them. You want to go beyond the customers' expectations and surprise them. A great example of this is Apple laptops and desktops. The great thing about them is that they are streamlined and easy to use, which satisfies the customers' requests. However, Apple goes a step further by offering free photo, music, and movie editing software, while putting in features such as saving a backup copy of the information on the computer every hour in case something happens. That delights the customer and that keeps them coming back to your product or service.

Studies have shown customers can tell you exactly what they want out of the products they understand and know, but they cannot always tell you what they want out of a new product they have not used, so it is up to you to provide them with what you think they will want but which they do not know they want.

The Measurement stage of DMADV will identify the Critical to Quality items that will be addressed in DMADV, and it will validate the metrics for the new process or product and create a measurement plan.

The problem with the Define stage is that you have what the customer wants to improve on for the product or process, but this is all in the voice of the customer. When the customer says: "I want a microwave that can also double as a toaster oven for space convenience and energy savings," then the company has to turn that request into something that can actually work and exist, and the first step in that process is the Measurement stage.

The project team will need to establish the metrics for each Critical to Quality item, converting it into a company requirement, or internal requirement. Data sources need to be created and the company also has to ask itself:

- What nonexistent data is currently needed?
- How will this data be gathered?
- What is the sample size of this data?
- What is the rational subgroup of the data that has to be gathered?

Customers are the key to the process, so you need to find a way to measure customer response and satisfaction to the product, which can be done through surveys and focus groups.

Chapter 14: Define and Measure

Following this, it is important to create a measurement plan:

- What is the definition of the operation of the metric?

- What data is going to be collected and who is going to collect it?

- Who will evaluate the results and how often will they do it?

- What are the requirements of the sample size?

- How will the methods be analyzed?

Once all of this is done, you can move on to the next stage of DMADV: Analyze.

Conclusion

Not surprisingly, the Design and Measure stage of DMADV resembles the same stages of DMAIC, but with less complexity. This is because you are not looking at a current process, measuring it, and determining how to make it better. Instead, you are working to create a whole new process, which means the creation of new measurements, new metrics, and new definitions of the product from what the customers want.

One important thing that needs to be pointed out is that the first stage of DMADV, like DMAIC, is getting the definition of what needs to be created or improved, not from shareholders or people in the company, but from people outside the company. They are the customers and they are the ones who dictate the trends and what the new big item will be. Those companies that take the time to talk to them and discover what they want are the companies that are going to succeed. Instead of creating a new product you think the customer will want, why not create a product based on what the customer has told you they want? Through surveys, feedback forms, focus groups, and more, you can discover exactly what the customer wants from future products.

This is what helps make Six Sigma successful, because in everything it does, it knows that in the end, it is the customer who benefits and the customer who makes the decisions, not the shareholders. This means that everything should be done to make the customer happy.

Chapter 15
Analyze

"The miracles of genius always rest on profound convictions which refuse to be analyzed."

-Ralph Waldo Emerson

Introduction

In DMAIC, the analysis of the process was a critical point. This is where the measurements were taken and the details of how to improve on the process were really laid down with cold, hard calculations. Simulations were run to see what was going to work best, and statistics were poured over to find the best options for improving the process given several beneficial results for various improvements.

The Analyze stage of DMADV works in a similar way, with the company and the project teams looking at how to create a product that will meet the Critical to Quality items that the customer has detailed to the company in the Define stage.

The Tasks

There are several tasks that need to be completed in the Analyze stage:

- Link design features to Critical to Quality items. This is done by the process expert.

- Determine the importance of the design feature. This is done by the black belts.

- Look at other companies who use similar processes as the benchmark. The entire project team does this.

- Define the standards of performance that will be set for the Critical to Quality items. The entire project team does this.

- Develop design concepts for the new process or product. This is done by the project team and process expert.

- Evaluate the different concepts created by the team and pick the best one. This is done by the black belts.

- Select the design concept that is the most promising. This is done by the project team.

- Sponsor the analyze gate review. This is done by the project sponsor.

To accomplish these tasks, the project team must do the following steps in the Analyze stage:

- Map out the Critical to Quality data to the design features outlined by the customers and the project team.

Chapter 15: Analyze

- Identify the high-level concepts for implementing the features.

- Choose the best concept to move forward with.

- Predict Critical to Quality performance level.

- Compare what is predicted to happen with the product to what the requirements are.

- Revise the design concept if needed.

Using Customer Demands to Design

After the customer has translated their demands to you, it is up to you to convert those demands into the requirements and the specifications of the project. This means when the customer says they want the microwave to be easier to use with leftovers, the designers and engineers have to determine the best option for a one-button feature that will cook the leftovers perfectly.

Remember, the purpose of creating specifications in the project, process, and product is to transmit the voice of the customer and their demands throughout the organization. When you are translating the customer demands into the design of the product, you will also have to make trade-offs for what the customer may not want. You may have had a feature on the microwave that allowed the customer to adjust the intensity level, but customers found this too complicated. So, to make room for the one-button features, you take out the intensity level and allow the microwave to just use an intensity level that is the average for that type of item (such as coffee, popcorn, and leftovers).

To turn demands into design concepts and to try and get everything that all the customers want into the product, you need to weigh the importance of everything. There are a number of ways to do this, including:

- Have customers assign the importance on a particular product on a scale of one to ten. An example of this is "How important is ease of use to you?" With one being the lowest and ten being the highest importance.

- Have customers evaluate a list of potential product offerings and indicate their preference for the product and whether they would buy it based on those features.

- Have the customer evaluate different items in pairs, choosing the one they think of as most important. This is an excellent way to eliminate unwanted features and products.

All of these come through in the process of a customer survey. There are several ways to do this, which will allow you to get the best understanding of what the customer wants.

This will also make the customer happy because they will feel as though they are having a say in the product and how it works, giving them greater satisfaction in the product because of a feeling they are being listened to.

The important thing to remember when you are creating customer surveys and feedback forms that will give you an indication of what the customer wants is that you cannot make it complicated. They must be easy to understand because that will give the customer their greatest amount of satisfaction.

Conclusion

One thing you will notice about the Analyze stage of the DMADV versus the Analyze stage of the DMAIC is that there are far fewer calculations. In fact, the DMADV Analyze stage is nearly completely dependent on talking to the customers because you are creating the new process based on what the customer wants out of their product.

Instead of calculating based on the measurements you have taken and then creating simulations and experiments to see what will improve the process the best, you are only talking to the customers. The simulations and experiments don't come in the Analyze stage with DMADV, but in the next stage: Design.

It is important to remember that when you are improving something, you have the data to figure out where to improve things. You know common-cause and special-cause factors that influence efficiency, and you know how to improve them by looking at accurate data.

When you are creating something new, you are not doing this. You are working toward designing a product or process that you have no data for. Therefore, all you can do is find out what the customer wants based on your different ideas for improvements and have the customer choose what is most important to them through surveys. This will allow your product to succeed because it is not so much the company analyzing things, but the customers.

The Six Sigma Manual

Chapter 16
Design and Verify

"Always design a thing by considering it in its next larger context — a chair in a room, a room in a house, a house in an environment, an environment in a city plan."

-Eliel Saarinen, Time, July 2, 1956

Introduction

This is where things change greatly from DMAIC to DMADV. The Design stage, which takes the place of the Improve stage of DMAIC, is where you begin to run your simulations and your experiments and put together the product that is going to work best for the customer, based completely on what they have analyzed for you in the previous stage.

There are several tasks that need to be completed in this stage, outlined as follows:

- Develop a design. This is done by the process expert and the project team.

- Determine what the Critical to Quality items will be of the design. This is done by the black belts.

- Revise the Critical to Quality predictions until they match the requirements as outlined by the customers. This is done by the process expert and the project team.

- Conduct a trial run with the design. This is done by the process owner and the process operator.

- Analyze the Critical to Quality results from the trial run. This is done by the black belts and green belts.

- Revise the design until the trial Critical to Quality items match the requirements from the customer. This is done by the process expert and the project team.

- Develop an implementation plan. This is done by the project team, process owner, and process operator.

- Sponsor the design gate review. This is done by the project sponsor.

As can be seen from these tasks, the Design stage is all about actually creating what the customer has outlined that they want and then putting it together for them.

Also, a great deal of the stage has to do with fine-tuning the process or product to ensure it matches exactly what the customer's requirements are. This is important, because no Six Sigma company wants to go through the process of creating something they think the customer will want, only to find out that as it reaches the market, no one wants to buy it.

That is a lot of wasted money and time.

Simulating the Processes

Simulations are the key to finding out if a process or product will function right in the real world. Simulations are great for a designer because they allow them to solve problems that may come up in the real world, without the time, cost, and effort of putting the product on the market without it being ready to go. The simulations use a model of the real-world system, allowing important questions to be answered, like 'Will this work for the customer?' and 'Will this stand up to the requirements set forth through customer surveys?'

To create the simulation model, the modeler must specify the scope of the model, as well as the level of detail that will be in the model. These are the factors that will have an impact on the ability of the model to test the product or process properly. The modeler wants to create, in a cheap way, a model of the real-world system that can answer the questions at a high level of detail. It needs to be closest to the real-world system, because only then will the simulation be accurate in the data it gives out. Several different simulation software modelers can be purchased by companies to see exactly how something will fare in the real-world system.

Managers and process operators love simulations because it gives them the ability to see how everything will perform, and often they will be surprised to see how the model of the system operates. This is because many people will focus on a task without understanding the role of that task in the grand scheme of things. Much like someone who inflates tires for a living, they may not have an appreciation for the role they play in assembling a car because they rarely see the product at the end of the assembly line.

Of course, to obtain good simulations, good data from the customers and current processes must be collected properly. Sometimes, getting this data can reveal problems in existing information systems, which then need to be cleared up to ensure proper data. This is another way in which Six Sigma improves a company through every nook and cranny.

Once simulations have been run, they can be applied to process changes, and that is where the real fun comes in. This, in turn, can create brand-new questions that need to be answered. For example, if simulations show that a promotion put on by the company will double the amount of computer orders, the question of how the current order staff will be able to handle that must be addressed. These are called unanticipated consequences because the teams had not looked at their possibility before the situation. People's lives are full of unanticipated consequences that they have to deal with when things change. When someone buys a large SUV, they may not have taken into consideration the consequences of paying high gas prices or the possibility that the SUV may not leave much room in their garage for the other vehicle that they own.

Unanticipated consequences are only a bad thing when they happen in the real world because a company did not run a simulation to see what would happen. The truth is, when you find unanticipated consequences during simulations, this gives you an excellent opportunity to improve the product and thereby improve the customers' satisfaction in that product.

You should never fear unanticipated consequences and should only see them as yet another way to make the product something the customers will love, thereby moving the company toward its Six Sigma goal.

Verifying Everything

Once the simulations have been run and the project team has addressed all the unanticipated consequences, then it is time to verify the plan and the process, which is the last stage of DMADV.

The tasks for the Verify stage are as follows:

- Develop a control plan that does the following:

  - Implements the recommendations outlined by the customer and team. This is done by the process owner.

  - Standardizes whatever is possible. This is done by the process owner.

  - Establishes the metrics of control. This is done by the process owner.

  - Develops a tool for metric collection. This is done by the black belts.

- Create a transition plan that does the following:

  - Trains the process operators. This is done by the process expert and process operators.

  - Monitors the process using a control plan. This is done by the process owner and black belt.

  - Changes the design if it is required to make it more in line with customer requirements. This is done by the process owner and process expert.

- Sponsor the project review by doing the following:

- Accept the deliverables of the project. This is done by the sponsor.

- Identify the lessons that are to be learned and the best practices of the project. This is done by the project sponsor and black belt.

- Plan for transferring the knowledge gained to other areas. This is done by the project sponsor and business leader.

Most of all, in the verify stage, you will do a pilot run of the process to see how it turns out. This is like a simulation, but it is actually done in the real world, and it will show you exactly how the company and product is going to fare with this. It can be done in a variety of ways, and when you are done, you move on to the full-scale operations. The pilot or trial run is giving select consumers the product and seeing how they like it. A full-scale operation is giving the world the product.

Conclusion

The Design and Verify stages are extremely important to the DMADV process. This is where you are designing everything and putting it to the test. You are going to be taking what the customer has asked of you and turning it into something they can actually see, experience, or use. This is where all the surveys, measurements, and definitions come into play because you are taking what the customer wants, what their desires are, and what they require and turning it into something tangible. This is not always the easiest task because it requires several simulations, fine-tuning, dealing with unexpected consequences, and more. However, when you are through these stages, you will be able to move on to providing customers with something they can use without any problems because your company has taken the steps to listen to them and create something that they want.

Section Conclusion

Six Sigma is full of tools that can be used to increase customer satisfaction and thereby increase efficiency and the profit margin. The two primary tools are DMAIC and DMADV, with DMAIC being used to improve what already exists, and DMADV being used to create something that the customers want. Companies are constantly evolving, and when they do not evolve, they die. It is the survival of the fittest, and it is true in nature and in life. Those companies that fail to use DMAIC and DMADV policies, even if they aren't in Six Sigma form, will eventually be left behind. Apple computers looked at what customers wanted and created it for them, and they still do. Now, they are beginning to make headway in the computer market and are becoming more popular with every passing year. Apple also created the iPhone and iPod, which were two things the public wanted. They listened to the public and translated their requirements into new products.

Polaroid was a dominant film company for decades and they were the go-to company for all things to do with cameras and film. However, they did not listen to what customers wanted, and as the world of cameras changed from film to digital, they were slowly left behind. Eventually, they were sold and portioned off, with their film division shutting down shop. This shows you what happens when you don't follow what customers want.

Following what customers want is what DMADV is all about. From defining their requirements, to measuring their requirements, and from analyzing their ideas and needs to designing and verifying the product they have requested, it is all about the customer. If the history of business has taught anything, it is that those companies that listen to the customers are the ones that survive into the future, while those that do not slowly disappear, like Polaroid is starting to.

Section 5
Lean Six Sigma

"A society in which consumption has to be artificially stimulated in order to keep production going is a society founded on trash and waste, and such a society is a house built upon sand."

-Dorothy L. Sayers, Creed or Chaos?

Section Introduction

One form of Six Sigma that is coming to the forefront is the concept of Lean Six Sigma. Lean Six Sigma is a set of principles and ideas that are meant for improving cycle times through the elimination of any type of waste. This allows you to distinguish between the value-added activities and the non-value-added activities. By removing non-value-added activities, you are able to improve cycle times, reduce waste, and increase the value of what the customer receives.

This has been shown to create huge benefits to the organizations that use it, with increasing production levels but by using less manpower. That then creates higher profit margins. The Lean Six Sigma philosophy itself came into being because of Taiichi Ohno of Toyota.

Lean Six Sigma was a revolutionary concept because it used the lean methodology of lowering waste, with the Six Sigma philosophy, creating Lean Six Sigma.

When you have something as incredibly efficient as Six Sigma, and combine it with something like the lean methodology, you are essentially creating the perfect storm.

Many companies will choose to use Lean Six Sigma throughout the DMAIC process because this is where you are going to be analyzing the data of the processes and determining how best to improve the process for maximum efficiency and customer satisfaction. There are few better ways to increase efficiency than through eliminating waste. As any business grad and manager will tell you, waste lowers efficiency greatly, and taking it out of the picture can increase waste by a large margin.

Through this section, you will learn about Six Sigma's new lean philosophy and how it can benefit your organization through the principles of Lean Six Sigma. Once through the section, you will know how the lean methodology can help your Six Sigma process. Like many, you will feel that lean methodologies and Six Sigma were simply made for each other, like two soul mates who finally cross paths.

The Six Sigma Manual

Chapter 17
The Principles of Lean

In Lean Six Sigma, there are seven different types of waste that make up the principles of the program. These are the forms of waste that were coined by Ohno in 1998 and called muda. The types of muda in business are:

1. Defects

2. Overproduction

3. Inventories

4. Unnecessary processing

5. Unnecessary movements of people

6. Unnecessary transport of goods

7. Waiting

These principles outline everything that is wrong with waste, and all of these contribute to lowering the company's ability to do business properly. As was discussed earlier, waste leads to lost money and lost money is lost profit. As well, that lost money can translate into further problems for the customer.

Defects

Defects are what you want to avoid in Six Sigma. The golden rule of the entire Six Sigma methodology is that efficiency level is 3.4 defects per one million units. What are defects? Essentially, defects are products you manufacture that you cannot sell or that you do sell, but causes lower customer satisfaction because the product does not work properly. This then leads to the customer bringing back the items in exchange for new ones, costing your company money.

When a company sells televisions, nothing can be perfect. There will be defects, but the point of Six Sigma is not to eliminate them, but to severely limit them. So, you have televisions that sell for $1,000 each. You send out one million of them, and if you are part of Lean Six Sigma, you only have three televisions come back. That means out of $1 billion in sales, you only lose $3,000. That is pretty good. However, if defects are a major problem for the company and it has 4,388 defects per one million units, which is horrible, then they will be losing $4,388,000 dollars. That is a lot of money.

Defects must be limited in Lean Six Sigma, almost more than anything else, because they are what will severely damage your relationship with the customer.

Overproduction

Often, a company will create too much of one product and then find out that it was not a popular product and that the public does not like the product. This then results in the company creating too much of something, spending too much money to create it, and not being able to sell it. That is a lot of lost money. If the overproduction of televisions is 30,000 units, the company loses $30,000,000 in products that people do not want to buy. They can be converted into something else, but the point is that they are lost for the profit the company wanted. Six Sigma is founded on learning about the customers you want to buy your products and the market in which they will buy the products or processes. As a result, not having researched enough, you will end up losing money. Overproduction doesn't even have to be with products. If you have a call center where 300 people are sitting around with nothing to do because you overestimated the potential call volume, then you are paying 300 extra salaries that you did not need to. That is waste and that is how overproduction can create vast amounts of waste, often more than defects do.

Inventories

This is a difficult one because many companies need to have inventories. These inventories can be finished goods or in-process goods, and it comes into play with overproduction. When a company is putting something together, they will use supplies that they have on hand. Sometimes, these supplies need to be used in a certain period and if they are not, that can lead to waste because the supplies can no longer be used.

This is a difficult waste to find and reduce because it is so entwined with putting the products and processes together. As a company, you do not want to be working on a product or process and find that there are not enough supplies in inventory to finish the supply so it meets demand.

Unnecessary Processing

Too many steps can create waste. This waste may not be in the sense of materials, but it can be in the sense of time. If a company has a production line that makes light bulbs, and after the bulbs are forged, they are washed, then counted, then washed again, there is waste. You can easily eliminate a part of that process in that they do not need to be washed again.

Earlier in the book, specialization was mentioned as a major contributor of waste, and it comes into play here. Too many departments create too much processing, which results in far too much waste.

Simplifying the production process will go an incredibly long way to reducing waste and ensuring that companies are able to operate with minimal waste because there is minimal processing going on.

Unnecessary Movement of People

Too many companies require people to move around the office or factory in an effort to do their job. If someone needs to fill out a service form for a customer, then walk across the office to scan it, then walk to the front desk to get the customer to sign it, then walk back to the scanner to scan it, then walk to a far off office to get the manager to sign it, the amount of movement is staggering. For larger corporations and factories, this movement can be even larger and that means larger waste.

For the customer sitting up at the front, the amount of movement being done eats into their time and that can lower customer satisfaction. Think of how everything could be streamlined if the scanner was located at the front and the employee did not need the signature of the boss unless the service order was over $10,000. Eliminating that step also comes into eliminating unnecessary processes.

Unnecessary Transport of Goods

This is one that happens on a daily basis. If someone or something has to be transported a long distance, it is going to create a lot of wasted time, and in business, time is money. A great example of this is the order processor that was addressed earlier. When someone calls in, they put the order into the system, then they need to send that order over to the individual who processes the order, then that has to be sent to the person who checks the order against inventory, before it finally gets back to the person who entered the order. The entire time the customer is on hold, and this lowers customer satisfaction greatly. Cross-training the individual so he or she can simply enter, process, and check the order all at their computer, eliminating the transport of the order.

Waiting

Tom Petty once sang that 'Waiting is the hardest part', and it really is. When a company is waiting on an order, it delays everything that the company does. Waiting eats into time, and that eats into money. Nothing can ruin a product like waiting. Look at it like a kitchen. You have three stations that all need to come together at the same time. The vegetables, meat, and sauce stations all need to get their pieces done so the order goes out all at once. If there is good communication, vegetables, meat, and sauce all get put on the plate at once, and the customer gets a hot and good meal.

However, what happens if vegetables are delayed by only two minutes? Now, meat has to hold off being put on the plate so it stays on the burner, on a lower setting, but it still gets past medium rare and becomes well done. At the same time, the sauce sits on its own burner to keep it warm, but it also begins to cook too long and thicken more than it should. Now, by the time that the vegetables are ready, they are looking great, but the meat is too tough and the sauce is too thick and a potential happy customer dislikes their meal and it is wasted.

The Laws of Lean Six Sigma

There are laws to everything. Gravity, physics, society, and sports all have laws that govern them, and so, too, does Lean Six Sigma.

The laws are as follows according to Lean Six Sigma for Service (2003):

- The Law of the Market: Customer Critical-to-Quality defines quality and is the highest priority for improvement. This is the foundation law of Lean Six Sigma.

- The Law of Flexibility: The velocity of any process is in proportion to the flexibility of the process.

- The Law of Focus: 20 percent of the activities in a process cause 80 percent of the delays.

- The Law of Velocity: The velocity of any process is inversely proportional to the amount of work-in-progress.

- The Law of Complexity and Cost: The complexity of the service or product generally adds more non-value-added costs and creates poor quality and slow process problems.

Conclusion

As can be seen in this chapter, Lean Six Sigma is all about waste. What many people do not realize is that there are several kinds of waste. Too often, companies will only look at defects, overproduction, and waiting as waste, but it goes well beyond that.

Waste can be as simple as someone walking too far to get a printout or as complicated as coordinating the shipment of hundreds of orders that all need to come together at the exact same time.

Waste is the enemy of everything Lean Six Sigma and regular Six Sigma stand for. Waste is created by defects, overproduction, inventories, unnecessary processing, unnecessary movement of people, unnecessary transport of goods, and waiting.

Looking at three of those points of waste, what can you notice? The word 'unnecessary' comes up quite a bit. This is because waste is unnecessary. That is what waste is defined as — something that cannot be used but could have been used. If you have a manufacturing process that creates a material that cannot be used in anything, that is not waste, it is a by-product. However, if you are making fabric circles, and you throw away the extra pieces of fabric that is not used, that is waste.

The most important thing a company can do to eliminate waste is to look at what it does and begin trimming the fat off things that do not contribute anything of consequence to the project.

These are items that are non-value-added because they add no value to the entire process. If you eliminate processes or transports that are valued for the process, you create problems. If you are shipping a product to a distribution center in Houston, when you are in Boston, and from Houston it goes to New York, that is unnecessary waste and it can be fixed.

That is the great thing about waste. It is not permanent, and it can be fixed, and all it takes is you eliminating the waste that is created.

Chapter 18
Becoming a Lean Business

"Habit and routine have an unbelievable power to waste and destroy."

-Henri de Lubac, Paradoxes

Introduction

Becoming a lean business is actually rather simple: you just need to eliminate the waste. While that is the easy part, actually taking the steps to do so is the hard part. Thankfully, there are plenty of ways that a company can eliminate waste and become more efficient, which helps it become more of a Six Sigma company as a result.

To become a Lean Six Sigma business, a company needs to understand some of the points of Six Sigma.

First, there is lead time and process speed. Lead time is how long it takes a company to deliver their product or service once the order is triggered. This could be delivering a order of towels from when the customer clicks 'Checkout' on the computer, or it could be the time between when the customer calls the help line to when their problem is solved.

To determine the lead time or process speed, use Little's Law:

Lead Time = Amount of Work-In-Process/Average Completion Rate.

This equation shows how long it will take a company to process an order by counting how much work is sitting around waiting to be finished and dividing it by the number of things can be completed in a week.

Another concept to understand is work-in-progress. As stated, it is the amount of work that is waiting to be completed. This could be 17 cars that are waiting for engines or 18 calls in the queue of people looking for help with their computer. This is the work that has been started but not finished.

The last important term to be covered here is Process Cycle Efficiency. This is the metric of waste for any service process, defined as a percentage of cycle time. To find Process Cycle Efficiency, just do the following calculation:

Process Cycle Efficiency = Value-Add Time/Total Lead Time

If you have a Process Cycle Efficiency of less than 10 percent it means there is a lot of non-value waste opportunity.

The Lean Lessons

There are lessons that have to be learned in order to become a Lean Six Sigma business. In all, there are five Lean Six Sigma lessons that should be learned for a business to operate with minimal waste and ensure its efficiency is as high as it can go.

Lesson One: Most Processes are Un-lean

Most of what companies do is un-lean — that is the simple truth. Often, as much as half of all the work the company does is non-value-added services. Nowhere is this more true than when a company is one that processes orders. A Lockheed Martin study

Chapter 18: Becoming a Lean Business

found that in the case of placing a purchase order and receiving the goods, 83 percent of what was done was non-value-added waste. This could be contacting vendors for a quote, checking stocks, correcting errors, and more. This is an astonishingly high amount of non-value-added pieces that slow down the overall efficiency of the entire company. Here are two flowcharts to show how Lean Six Sigma can speed up your business if you simply look for the non-value-added services and eliminate them.

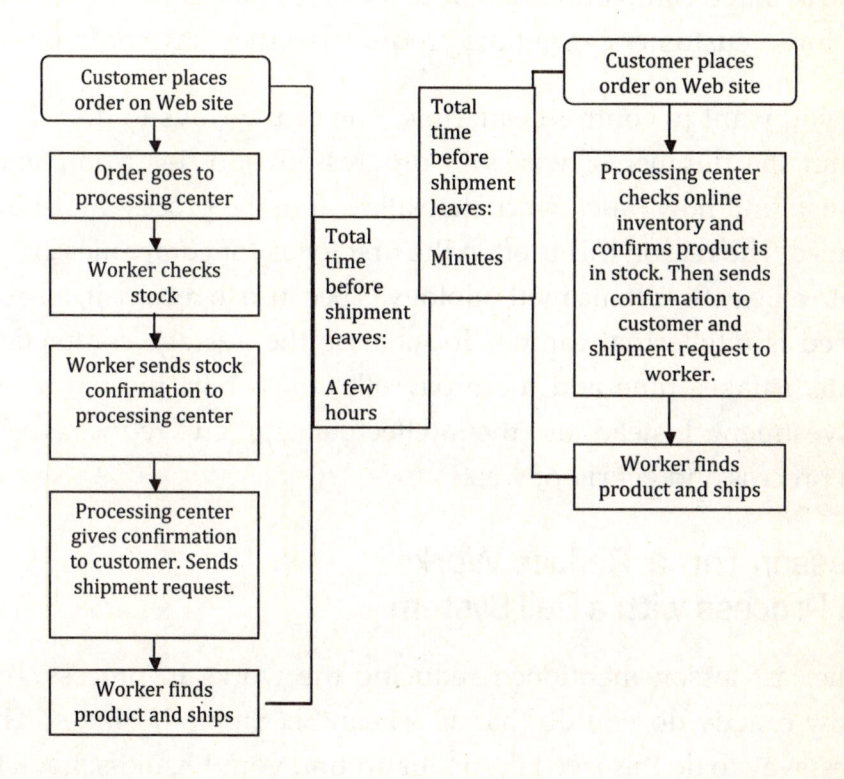

```
Customer places              Customer places
order on Web site            order on Web site
      ↓                             ↓
Order goes to        Total    Processing center
processing center    time     checks online
      ↓              before   inventory and
Worker checks        shipment confirms product is
stock                leaves:  in stock. Then sends
      ↓              Minutes  confirmation to
Worker sends stock            customer and
confirmation to               shipment request to
processing center             worker.
      ↓                             ↓
Processing center             Worker finds
gives confirmation            product and ships
to customer. Sends
shipment request.
      ↓
Worker finds
product and ships

Total time before shipment leaves: A few hours
```

This flowchart is a simple representation, but it shows exactly where items can be eliminated to speed things up. Rather than sending a request to the worker to check stock, simply have an automated system for stock checking. This eliminates several steps and does not require the worker to find the order and send a confirmation. The system can now check the stock and alert the worker to put the order in within minutes, even seconds.

This is the first lesson of Lean Six Sigma. Most of what a company does are non-value-added items, and these are all things that can be eliminated to speed up the process and eliminate waste.

Lesson Two: Always Reduce Works in Process

Earlier in the section, you learned about works in process and lead time. Works in process have a big effect on Lead Time. Along with the average completion rate, it determines how long it will take before a customer can get the product that they have ordered.

If you want to control Lead Time, one of the ways to do it is to limit the number of works in progress. To do this, companies must limit how much work they allow into the process at certain times. The reason this is often the first focus for companies going into a Lean Six Sigma methodology is because to reduce it, all you need is intellectual capital. To increase the average completion rate, it takes time and more payroll, which hurt the return on investment. Instead, use the intellectual capital to reduce works in process and get rid of waste.

Lesson Three: Reduce Works in Process with a Pull System

The last lesson mentioned reducing the works in process, but how exactly do you do that as a Lean Six Sigma business? The best way to do this is to take a tour around your business. Look to see if there are long lists of things people have to do, is their inbox full, how many unanswered e-mail orders are they dealing with? If it is your own office, look at these and find ways to reduce these items, because all of them represent something someone wants of you, which are works in process.

Looking at Little's Laws, if you have 39 order requests in your inbox, and you can complete 17 orders a day, it will take you 2.29

Chapter 18: Becoming a Lean Business

days to finish all of this. That is a lot of time when people are waiting on their orders.

This is where you use the pull system, because the 2.29-day turnaround does not start until the request or quote enters the process from you opening it to you completing it. To use a pull system, you have to make deliberate decisions as to when work enters the process. You cannot simply go on the philosophy of first-come, first-serve with this. Instead, look at the requests you have. If you have 39 of them, and they vary in complexity, you can then change how quickly you do everything. If 22 requests for quotes can be completed two hours and the other 17 can be completed in one day, then you will want to get the 22 requests out quickly, since it will only take you a few days.

You should also look at each potential request in the system through three criteria:

1. The difficulty
2. The advantage to the company
3. The gross profit dollars

Naturally, you want to ensure that you get the best advantage for the company. You will work on the projects that have the least difficulty for you, but the most advantage and gross profit for the company.

To create a pull system that will work, use these steps:

1. Identify the service level you hope to achieve. This can be done by asking your customers in a survey what they expect out of the company for service.

2. Determine the completion rate of the workgroup who will handle this process.

3. Determine the maximum works in process using Little's Law.

4. Don't allow any more work into the process when you reach the maximum works in process.

5. Pull all incoming work into an input buffer.

6. Develop a system to figure out when incoming work can be put into the process.

7. Continue to improve on the process to improve completion rates.

Lesson Four: The Better the Process Efficiency, the Better the Opportunity

Most companies operate at 5 percent process cycle efficiency. This means that they spend 95 percent of their time waiting. This is horrible, because that means 95 percent of the money spent on employees and time is wasted. For a company, that can be a disaster on the pocketbook of the corporation.

Most companies want to have over 20 percent process cycle efficiency, which is what most Lean Six Sigma companies strive for. The best way to reduce this is to map out how long it takes everybody to do their job. You want to find out how you can keep the process moving, without anyone waiting for materials, people, or something else.

Lesson Five: 20 Percent of Activities Cause 80 Percent of the Delay

The goal of Lean Six Sigma is speed. Speed comes from zero waste. When you look at the body of someone, they may have a lot of wasted muscle, wasted fat, and wasted ligaments. They have not done what they could to maintain it. So, in a marathon against someone who operates their body at peak efficiency, they will lose completely. Why? The reason is because the waste of the body lowers efficiency and that means less speed.

People will often call the processes that eat up 80 percent of the time 'time traps.' The goal of a Lean Six Sigma company is to speed things up by eliminating any of the waste items that were outlined in this section. When you have someone who has to walk to the scanner to get something scanned while a customer waits, that is a delay. Putting the scanner where the customer will be eliminates that. This is all about delay. Delay is the enemy of Lean Six Sigma. Take a look at your company and find out what can be eliminated to get rid of delay. If you can, talk to the people who work at your company and find out from them what they think adds to their job and can be eliminated. You will be shocked by the number of things that can be fixed to improve the speed of your company and get it to the point where it can be called Six Sigma.

Lean Tips

Those five rules are important to helping your company become a Lean Six Sigma company, but there are also some other tips that can be used to make it even more efficient, with little waste.

1. Find the value of existing and potential customers.

2. Find out how work flows to create a value stream of that work. Determine how the information moves through the process to support it.

3. Distribute work evenly and balance the process.

4. Standardize the process; do not specialize. The more people can do, the less worry there is about something shutting down because no one can handle the task.

5. Eliminate the activities that are there 'in case' something happens.

6. Nurture good relationships with your suppliers.

7. Create autonomation. This is a word from Taiichi Ohno, which describes a production system that mimics the human nervous system, including being able to automatically adjust to new conditions.

Conclusion

Your company needs to be the Road Runner, not Wile E. Coyote. This is because the Road Runner is all about speed and getting where it wants to go without any hiccups. Wile E. Coyote only suffers setback after setback and never gets to its goal.

As a Six Sigma company, you need to be speedy and efficient. This comes through in the process of eliminating waste in Lean Six Sigma. You will be able to work hard to get rid of all those things that don't belong in the company. Whether it is someone walking too far for a form or too many works in process, you can turn your company into a Lean Six Sigma business by just eliminating the dreaded waste.

The lessons talked about here are a good way to do that, and by applying what you know about Six Sigma to the concept of being lean, you will be able to get rid of the waste that troubles your company so much.

Chapter 19
Kaizen Methodology

"Our rulers will best promote the improvement of the nation by strictly confining themselves to their own legitimate duties, by leaving capital to find its most lucrative course, commodities their fair price, industry and intelligence their natural reward, idleness and folly their natural punishment, by maintaining peace, by defending property, by diminishing the price of law, and by observing strict economy in every department of the state. Let the Government do this: the People will assuredly do the rest."

-Thomas Babington Macaulay

Introduction

An interesting concept that has come out of Japan is KAISEN. This philosophy centers around continuous improvement. For those in Japan, it goes beyond the workplace and is a part of their lives, while in North America, it centers on the improvement at the workplace.

This approach focuses attention on improving everyone in the company. To do this, it focuses on the small improvements that can produce changes that are just as big as Six Sigma changes.

KAIZEN does not change fundamental systems, but simply works to optimize the systems that are already there. Under KAIZEN, all jobs in the organization fall under two components: process improvement and process control. You have learned about process control as a way to maintain a Six Sigma process that has been implemented, while process improvement is going through the work to get the highest efficiency out of a process in the company.

Six Sigma is about radical changes and innovations to the company, while KAIZEN is not.

The idea for KAIZEN can be best described through a cycle created by Deming and Stewhart.

- First, someone has to have an idea for doing the job better.
- Experiments need to be conducted to investigate the idea.
- The results need to be evaluated.
- If the desired results work, then the process of the company needs to be changed.

According to the KAIZEN Institute, the hierarchy of how a company is involved in KAIZEN is as follows:

Top Management

- Must be determined to introduce KAIZEN as the corporate strategy.
- Provide support and direction by allocating resources for KAIZEN.
- Establish a policy for KAIZEN.

- Help realize the goals of KAIZEN through policy deployment and audits.

- Must build systems, procedures, and structures that work with the philosophy of KAIZEN.

Middle Management

- Deploy and implement the goals of KAIZEN as directed by top management, through cross-functional management.

- Use KAIZEN in functional capabilities.

- Establish, maintain, and upgrade standards and staff.

- Make employees conscious of KAIZEN through training programs.

- Help employees develop the skills they need for problem-solving in KAIZEN.

Supervisors

- Use KAIZEN in functional roles.

- Create plans for KAIZEN and provide worker guidance.

- Improve communication with workers to keep morale high.

- Support small group activities and implement individual suggestion systems.

- Provide KAIZEN suggestions.

- Introduce discipline in KAIZEN workshops.

Workers

- Engage in KAIZEN through suggestion systems and group activities.

- Practice discipline in the workshops.

- Engage in self-development to become better problem solvers in the company.

- Enhance skills and job performance experience with cross-training opportunities.

Conclusion

Clearly, looking at the sections in this chapter, improving oneself on a continuous basis is an integral part of the KAIZEN philosophy. As stated, you will have everyone in the company, no different than Six Sigma, working toward a common goal of improving themselves, and by extension, the company. This will help them become better employees, help you become a better boss, and push the company to the point where it can be considered highly efficient.

If you are on board with Six Sigma, then going the extra mile with KAIZEN should not be that difficult. You are already working to improve your company and its processes, and that is what KAIZEN is all about. So really, you are only taking a few extra steps to get to that point and become more efficient by encouraging employees to be constantly improving themselves and the company as a whole.

Section Conclusion

Lean Six Sigma was described in this book as the perfect storm. It was called this because it takes the lean methodology of eliminating waste in all its forms, and combines it with Six Sigma, which strives to be highly efficient. What hurts efficiency more than waste? When a company is constantly dealing with high levels of waste, waiting, unnecessary activities, and more, how does it get the processes done to make it successful?

When a customer has to wait two weeks for an order because of inefficient and unnecessary non-value-added steps to the order and shipping process, what do you think that does to customer satisfaction?

As was outlined before, waste comes in the following forms:

1. Defects
2. Overproduction
3. Inventories
4. Unnecessary processing
5. Unnecessary movements of people
6. Unnecessary transport of goods
7. Waiting

When these types of waste rear their ugly heads, it is up to companies to find ways to get rid of that waste, and that comes to Lean Six Sigma. Lean Six Sigma, the blend of lean methodology and Six Sigma, improves on the process of making a process better.

This may seem odd to say, but it means that Six Sigma improves on how a company makes something better. Improvements on improving is key to long-term success. All of this is done by taking out the waste that hurts processes. Often, the one thing companies have to do to become efficient enough to be called Six Sigma is to eliminate waste.

Remember what was said before, about how 20 percent of the activities create 80 percent of the waste. The thing you have to do as the business leader is find those activities and find out how you can make them much more efficient and lower waste by as much as 70 to 75 percent. Doing this will increase productivity, increase efficiency, and make customers happy.

When customers are happy, they will be more inclined to purchase products from the company and the company will continue making money. It is a win-win situation for everyone. The company makes more money for being more efficient, and the customer gains satisfaction in the service or product they received from the company.

In the next section, the various other types of Six Sigma strategies will be looked at. These are the strategies that are not used anywhere near as much as the DMAIC and DMADV strategies, but they are important enough to be mentioned and they may help your company in the future.

Before moving on, remember: Waste is bad.

Section 6

Other Six Sigma Models

"In anything at all, perfection is finally attained, not when there is no longer anything to add, but when there is no longer anything to take away."

- Antoine De Saint-Exupery

Section Introduction

Six Sigma is anything but a one-trick pony. It offers a variety of solutions and methods for turning a company into a perfect efficiency machine. Some of these work great for some companies, while others do not.

The important thing is to know about them and know how they can help your company become successful as a Six Sigma company. Doing this will turn your company into one that is envied in the industry and one that customers will want to come to.

Throughout this book, you have seen the various ways companies will implement Six Sigma process improvement and creation projects in the form of DMAIC and DMADV. In both of those, the DMA stands for Design, Measurements, and Analyze. The IC stands for Improve and Control, while the DV stands for Design and Verify.

These are the two ways that companies will most often go for improvement, but what about those other types?

There are six more big Six Sigma models that you need to be aware of so that you can use them if you feel that the time is right:

1. MAIC
2. DCCDI
3. DCDOV
4. DMADOV
5. IDOV
6. CDOV

Section 6: Other Six Sigma Models

These models use some of the similar stages in DMAIC and DMADV, with some using all but one or two.

MAIC

This model is nearly similar to the original DMAIC, except that the process of Define has been removed, making the measurement stage the first one. This would be used if you already know the problem that has to be fixed in the process and you need to begin right with the measurement stage. This is rarely used, since DMAIC provides so much more in terms of what a company can do to understand and solve a problem.

DCCDI

This is a relatively new model for Six Sigma, popularized by Geoff Tennant. It is defined as the following stages:

- Define: The project goals are defined here for what the process must achieve.

- Customer: The analysis of what the customer wants is done at this point.

- Concept: Ideas are developed, then looked at, and reviewed before being selected.

- Design: The concept that has been selected is then designed and tested to see if it will meet the requirements of the customer and the business.

- Implementation: This is done when the design has proven to be successful and the product or service is ready to be commercialized by the company.

DCDOV

This model was created by Uniworld, using some of the same stages seen in other Six Sigma models, just in different orders. The stages are as follows:

- Define: Defining the requirements of the improvement to the process or the new product or service that the customer will want.

- Concept: Ideas are developed, then looked at, and reviewed before being selected.

- Design: The concept that has been selected is then designed and tested to see if it will meet the requirements of the customer and the business.

- Optimize: The product or service is created with a robust design, the reliability is estimated, and the Six Sigma policies are put in to optimize it and predict the quality level.

- Verify: The product or service is tested to ensure it is ready for full-market distribution.

IDOV

This is a popular new model of Six Sigma that has appeared in North America. Its stages are as follows:

- Identify: The Voice of the Customer and the Critical to Quality requirements are found and assigned to quality targets.

- Design: The system concepts and Critical to Quality items are transferred to functions, and the Critical to Quality items are designed.

- Optimize: The product or service is created with a robust design, the reliability is estimated, and the Six Sigma policies are put in to optimize it and predict the quality level.

- Validate: This is the testing phase for the prototypes to assess the performance and reliability of the product or service. If needed, a redesign is possible.

DMADOV

This Six Sigma model is used to develop new processes or products at high quality levels or if a process that is already in the company needs more than just an incremental improvement. The stages are as follows:

- Define: Defining the requirements of the improvement to the process or the new product or service that the customer will want.

- Measurement: The metrics are determined to find out what works best for the analysis of what the customer wants and the translation of that into a product or service or improvement on a process.

- Analyze: Here, the options of what the customer needs and the creative solutions that will work for them are devised.

- Design: The system concepts and Critical to Quality items are transferred to functions, and the Critical to Quality items are designed.

- Optimize: The product or service is created with a robust design, the reliability is estimated, and the Six Sigma policies are put in to optimize it and predict the quality level.

- Verify: The product or service is tested to ensure it is ready for full-market distribution.

CDOV

This model is used when the concept needs to be created before anything else can be done. This one does not use analyzing or measurements, and dives right into making a prototype.

- Concept: Ideas are developed, then looked at, and reviewed before being selected.

- Design: The system concepts and Critical to Quality items are transferred to functions, and the Critical to Quality items are designed.

- Optimize: The product or service is created with a robust design, the reliability is estimated, and the Six Sigma policies are put in to optimize it and predict the quality level.

- Verify: The product or service is tested to ensure it is ready for full-market distribution.

Section Conclusion

These models are used on occasion, but since they use most of the same stages as the two primary models, DMAIC and DMADV, they are not always used. Many have come into being because companies have chosen to create their own Six Sigma models rather than use the standard ones. For example, CDOV may be for a company that works primarily in research and development. For them, wasting time with customers they may not deal with would lower efficiency, so they simply dive into creating the concepts that they will design, optimize, and verify later on.

Maybe one of the models will work for you, or you may decide to create your own.

Conclusion

Is it any easier to understand Six Sigma after reaching this point in the book? This is a revolutionary way of doing things that some of the greatest companies in the world have latched onto to help them be more efficient and succeed further than their competition.

Six Sigma is something every company should think about implementing if they want to succeed in the world of business. The best analogy for this is to look at the animal kingdom.

An animal such as a wildebeest, for example, is slow and lumbering, not terribly efficient, and takes time for it to go anywhere. Its speed is lacking, and it's not the most intelligent of animals. This is like so many other plodding-along companies that only do what they need to so they can make a profit, but not pushing themselves or their employees any further.

Then you have the cheetah. This is an incredibly efficient creature that is able to run faster than any other animal on the planet. Through this efficiency, it can run down prey in an astonishingly quick amount of time. That is the Six Sigma company. They are efficient, speedy, and nothing is wasted.

Think about the efficiency rate of a company that uses Six Sigma: 3.4 defective units per one million. Then look at what defines the other forms of Sigma.

SIGMA LEVEL	DEFECTS PER MILLION	EFFICIENCY PERCENTAGE
Six	3.4	99.99966 percent
Five	233	99.9767 percent
Four	6,210	99.379 percent
Three	66,807	93.3193 percent
Two	308,537	69.1463 percent
One	690,000	31 percent

Six Sigma has so much efficiency that its margin for error from Six to Five Sigma is only 0.02296 percent. If your company only has 230 more defects per million, it falls below the Six Sigma guidelines. In fact, if you have more than 94 percent efficiency, you are only a Four Sigma. Even if you have more than 90 percent efficiency, you are only a Three Sigma.

Many companies are happy with 93.3193 percent efficiency, but there are companies that want more. If you have read this book, that means you want more efficiency and you want to expand beyond what others think is 'acceptable.'

Through this book, you have seen Six Sigma is something every person in the company has to be a part of. From the champions of the project, to the yellow belts who spend their time trying to get the processes to work effectively on the ground level of the company, Six Sigma is company-wide.

Everyone needs to be on board with Six Sigma or it is doomed to failure. It is like a huge trireme where everyone is rowing. If there is one person rowing in the opposite direction, it is going to screw up the entire process and no one is going to get anywhere.

Even looking at the two main methodologies of Six Sigma, DMAIC and DMADV, you can see how everybody needs to work together to get things moving.

From those who design the solutions and improvements, to those who measure them and analyze them, even to the point where the solution and improvement is being used in the company by the employees, everyone is taking part.

Speaking of parts, who is the most important part of the Six Sigma world for a company? If you said the customer, then you are right.

The customer is the entity that Six Sigma works for. Everything that a company does in the Six Sigma process is to raise customer satisfaction and happiness. When a customer does not get a defective product because defective products are kept to an incredible minimum, then they are happy. They end up buying more from the company, and even when something does go wrong, the customer service system has been fine-tuned and improved so much that they don't even have to worry about not getting help. Six Sigma is about being proactive for the customer, not reactive, so the company will do everything it can to ensure the customer is happy with what they buy and in the unlikely event they get one of the 3.4 defective units out of one million, then they can get the help they need to fix the problem.

Leaving this book, you should understand that Six Sigma is something you can apply throughout your company, and even to your own life. Six Sigma is about improvement and working to make something better. It is about not settling for what you already have and not thinking about making it better. That is a Two Sigma philosophy.

You can keep improving yourself as well, bettering yourself and bettering your company. If you feel you could improve on something about you, then do it. It is a lot easier than improving an entire company, and it is good training for when you do put Six Sigma in the workplace.

Take what you have learned here to your company and begin becoming a company that is a leader in the world. You need to ask yourself if you want to be a better company or if you want to go away and be forgotten, like Polaroid. The choice is yours, but if you choose correctly, then your Six Sigma journey will begin and you will move on to becoming the leader of a company that you can be proud of.

Join the Six Sigma Revolution

Six Sigma Glossary

Courtesy of Six Sigma Qualtec

Abscissa - The horizontal axis of a graph.

Acceptance Region Alpha Risk - The region of values for which the null hypothesis is accepted.

A/D Transducer - A device that converts analog data into digital form.

Algorithm - 1. A set of rules or processes to find a problem's solution in a certain number of steps. 2. Detailed procedures for giving instructions to a computer.

Alpha Risk - The probability of accepting the alternate hypothesis when, in reality, the null hypothesis is true.

Alternate Hypothesis - A tentative explanation which indicates that an event does not follow a chance distribution.

Analog - The representation of numerical quantities by means of physical variables, such as translation, rotation, voltage, or resistance; contrasted with digital.

Analog Signal - An analog signal is a continuously variable representation of a physical quantity, property, or condition such as pressure, flow, temperature, etc. The signal may be transmitted as pneumatic, mechanical, or electrical energy.

Application Memory- The memory which stores the programmed instructions and data to control a specific machine or process. Application memory is often random access memory.

Arithmetic Logic Baud Rate- A computer chip which computes mathematical functions.

Assignable Cause - A source of variation which is non-random; a change in the source ("VITAL FEW" variables) will produce a significant change of some magnitude in the response (dependent variable). An assignable cause is often signaled by an excessive number of data points outside a control limit and/or a non-random pattern within the control limits. It can also be a source of variation that does not seem natural, which is economical to eliminate easily.

Assignable Variations - Variations in data which can be attributed to specific causes.

Atmospheric Pressure - The barometric reading of pressure exerted by the atmosphere; at sea level 14.7 lbs. per sq. in. or 29.92 in. of mercury.

Attribute - A characteristic that may take on only one value, e.g. 0 or 1.

Attribute Data - Numerical information at the nominal level; the division of this is not meaningful. Data which represents the frequency of occurrence within some discrete category, e.g., 42 solder shorts.

Background Variables - Variables which are of no experimental interest and are not held constant. The background variables are often seen as unneeded, pointless or a detriment to the overall data.

Back-Up-Battery - A battery which is available to maintain memory contents in the event of primary power failure.

Baud Rate - The rate of a unit of signal speed equal to the number of code elements (pulses and spaces) per second or twice the number of pulses per second.

Beta Risk - The probability of accepting the null hypothesis when, in reality, the alternate hypothesis is true.

Bimetal - A bonded laminate consisting of two strips of dissimilar metals; the bond is usually a stable metallic bond produced by coroiling or diffusion bonding; the composite material is used most often as an element for detecting temperature changes by means of differential thermal expansion in the two layers.

Bimetallic Thermometer Element - A temperature-sensitive strip of metal (or other configuration) made by mechanically bonding or mechanically joining two dissimilar strips of metal together in such a manner that small changes in temperature will cause the composite assembly to distort elastically and produce a predictable deflection; the element is designed to take advantage of the fact that different metals have different coefficients of thermal expansion.

Bit - The smallest unit of information that can be recognized by a computer.

Black Belt - The leader of the team responsible for applying the Six Sigma process.

Blocking Variables - A relatively homogenous set of conditions within which different conditions of the primary variables are compared. This is used to keep background variables from changing the primary variables.

Calibration- Determination of the experimental relationship between the quantity being measured and the output of the device that measures it; where the quantity measured is obtained through a recognized standard of measurement.

Cascade Control - 1. A control system composed of two loops where the set point of one loop (the inner loop) is controlled by the output of the second loop (the outer loop). 2. A control technique that incorporates a master and a slave loop. The master loop control the primary control parameters and establishes the slave4oop set point. The purpose of the slave loop is to reduce the effect of disturbances on the primary control parameter and to improve the dynamic performance of the loop.

Causative - Effective as a cause.

C Charts - Charts which display the number of defects per sample.

Champion-Person responsible for the logistical and business aspects of a Six Sigma project. Champions select and scope projects that are aligned with the corporate strategy, choose and mentor the right people for the project, and remove barriers to ensure the highest levels of success.

Celsius - A scale for temperature measurement based on the definition of 0 C and 100 C as the freezing point and the boiling point, respectively, of water at standard pressure.

Central Tendency - Numerical average, e.g., mean, median, and mode; center line on a statistical process control chart.

Center Line - The line on a statistical process control chart which represents the characteristic's central tendency.

Centigrade- A non-preferred term formerly used to designate the scale now referred to as the Celsius scale.

Central Processing Unit (CPU) - Made up of one or more microprocessors and associated components. The CPU controls system activities including interpretation and execution of programs. It has an arithmetic logic unit (ALU), timing and control circuitry, accumulator, scratch-pad memory, program counter, address stack, and instruction register.

Confidence Level - The probability that a random variable x lies within a defined interval.

Confidence Limits- The two values that define the confidence interval.

Configuration - The arrangement of software-based function blocks in a controller. The configuration determines what functions the controller can perform and in what order.

Confounding - Allowing two or more variables to vary together so that it is impossible to separate their unique effects.

Consumers Risk - Probability of accepting a lot when, in fact, the lot should have been rejected (see BETA RISK).

Continuous Data - Numerical information at the interval of ratio level; In this case, subdivision is meaningful; can assume any number within an interval, e.g., 14.652 amps.

Continuous Random Variable - A random variable which can assume any value continuously in some specified interval.

Control Chart - A graphical rendition of a characteristic's performance across time in relation to its natural limits and central tendency.

Control Specifications - Specifications called for by the product being manufactured.

Controlled Variable - 1. The variable which the control

system attempts to keep at the set point value. The set point may be constant or variable. 2. The part of a process you want to control (flow, level, temperature, pressure, etc.). 3. A process variable which is to be controlled at some desired value by means of manipulating another process variable.

Cutoff Point - The point which partitions the acceptance region from the reject region.

D/A Transducer - A device that converts a digital signal into a proportional analog voltage or current.

Dashboard - A set of metrics, usually not more than five or six, that provide an "at-a-glance" summary of a Six Sigma project's status. Every participant in a Six Sigma deployment -- from the CEO to a factory floor worker -- should have his or her own dashboard with function- and level-appropriate data summaries.

Degrees of Freedom - The number of independent measurements available for estimating a population parameter.

Density Function - The function which yields the probability that a particular random variable takes on any one of its possible values.

Dependent Variable - A Response Variable; e.g., y is the dependent or "Response" variable where $Y=f(X1...XN)$ variable.

Derivative Control - In process instrumentation, control action in which the output is proportional to the rate of change of the input.

Deviation - The difference between the value of a specific variable and some desired value, usually a process set point.

Differential Pressure - 1. The difference between the pressure at any two defined points. 2. The static pressure difference generated by the primary device when there is no difference in elevation between the upstream gage and the downstream gage.

Differential Pressure Transmitter - Any of several transducers designed to measure the pressure difference between two points in a process and transmit a signal proportional to this difference, without regard to the absolute pressure at either point.

Digital Signal - A discrete or discontinuous signal; often one whose various states are discrete intervals apart.

Discrete Random Variable - A random variable which can assume values only from a definite number of discrete values.

Distributions - Tendency of large numbers of observations to group themselves around some central value with a certain amount of variation or "scatter" on either side.

E/I Transducer - A device that linearly converts a voltage signal into a current signal.

Elbow Meter - A pipe elbow that is used as a flow measurement device by placing a pressure tap at both the inner and outer radii and measuring the pressure differential caused by the differences in flow velocity between the two flow paths.

Execution Sequence Number - The order in which the controller executes function blocks.

Executive Program - The program in the PLC which contains instructions to direct the CPU in its execution of system activities.

Experiment - A test under defined conditions to determine an unknown effect; to illustrate or verify a known law; to test or establish a hypothesis.

Experimental Error - Variation in observations made under identical test conditions. Also called residual error. The amount of variation which cannot be attributed to the variables included in the experiment.

Feedback - 1. Process signal used in control as a measure of response to control action. 2. The part of a closed loop system which automatically brings back information about the condition under control.

Feedback Control - An error driven control system in which the control signal to the actuators is proportional to the difference between a command signal from the process variable being controlled.

Feedforward Control - A method of control that compensates for a disturbance before its effect is felt in the output. It is based on a model that relates the output to the input where the disturbance occurs. In distillation, the disturbances are usually feed rate and feed compositions. Steady-state feedforward models are usually combined with dynamic compensation functions to set the manipulative variables and combined with feedback adjustments (trim) to correct for control model-accuracy constraints.

Fiber Optics - A medium that uses light conducted through glass or plastic fibers for data transmission.

Fixed Effects Model - Experimental treatments are specifically selected by the researcher. Conclusions only apply to the factor levels considered in the analysis. Inferences are restricted to the experimental levels.

Flowrate - The quantity of fluid that moves through a pipe or channel within a given period of time.

Flowmeter - An instrument used to measure linear, nonlinear, or volumetric flow rate or discharge rate of a fluid flowing in a pipe. Also known as a fluid meter.

Flownozzle - A type of differential pressure producing element having a contoured entrance; characterized by its ability to be mounted between flanges and have a lower permanent pressure loss than an orifice plate.

Fluctuations - Variances in data, which are caused by a large number of, minute variations or differences.

Frequency Distributions - The pattern or shape formed by the group of measurements in a distribution.

Function Blocks - Programming tools that represent steps in a control strategy.

Gage - (alternate spelling of Gauge) is a device or process by which measurements are taken.

Gage R&R - (Gage Repeatability and Reproducibility) this is a statistical tool that measures the accounts the amount of variation in the measurement system from the device used, the people taking the measurement, the interaction between the device and the person and the error seen from the parts.

Green Belt - An individual who supports the implementation and application of Six Sigma tools by way of participation on project teams.

Histogram - Vertical display of a population distribution in terms of frequencies; a formal method of plotting a frequency distribution.

Homogeneity of Variance - The variances of the groups being contrasted are equal (as defined by statistical test of significant difference).

Human Factors - Human capabilities and limitations to the design and organization of the work environment. Primarily attributed to errors, but also a consideration in the design of workflow and processes. The study of human factors can help identify operations susceptible to human error and improve working conditions to reduce fatigue and inattention.

Hydrostatic Head - The pressure created by the height of a liquid above a given point.

Independent Variable - A controlled variable; a variable whose value is independent of the value of another variable.

I/E Transducer - A device that linearly converts a current signal into a voltage signal.

I/O Rack Memory - Chassis for mounting computer I/O modules. May be local or remote from CPU/memory unit.

I/P Transducer - A device that linearly converts electric current into gas pressure.

Input Module - This module accepts analog or digital voltage and current signal from field devices. An analog-to-digital converter inside the module changes analog input signals into a digital format to be interpreted by the CPU. The input module also conditions the signal through sampling and filtering.

Instability - Unnaturally large fluctuations in a pattern.

Instrument - A device for measuring the value of an observable attribute; the device may merely indicate the observed value, or it may also record or control the value.

Instrumentation - Any system of instruments and associated devices used for detecting, signaling, observing, measuring, controlling, or communicating attributes of a physical object or process.

Integral Control Action - Control action in which the output is proportional to the time integral of the input; i.e., the rate of change of output is proportional to the input.

Interaction - The tendency of two or more variables to produce an effect in combination which neither variable would produce if acting alone.

Internal Energy - Ability of a working fluid to do its work based on the arrangement and motion of its molecules.

Interval - Numeric categories with equal units of measure but no absolute zero point, i.e., quality scale or index.

Kelvin - Metric unit for thermodynamic temperature. An absolute temperature scale in which the zero point is defined as absolute zero (the point where all spontaneous molecular activity ceases) and the scale divisions are equal to the scale divisions in the Celsius system; in the Kelvin system, the scale divisions are not referred to as degrees as they are in other temperature measurement systems but as kelvins; 0 C equals approximately 273.16 K.

Kinetic Energy - The energy of a working fluid caused by its motion.

Laser - Light Amplification by Stimulated Emission of Radiation. It is a source of EM radiation generally in the IR, visible, or UV bands and is characterized by small divergence, coherence, monochromaticity, and high collimation.

Latent Heat - Heat that does not cause a temperature change.

LED - Light Emitting Diode.

Limit Function - Action which sets a high or low limit on any signal within the controller.

Line Charts - Charts used to track the performance without relationship to process capability or control limits.

Lower Control Limit - A horizontal dotted line plotted

on a control chart which represents the lower process limit capabilities of a process.

Manipulated Variable - 1. In a process that is desired to regulate some condition, a quantity or a condition that is altered by the control in order to initiate a change in the value of the regulated condition. 2. The part of the process which is adjusted to close the gap between the set point and the controlled variable.

Manometer - A gage for measuring pressure or a pressure difference between two fluid chambers. A U-tube manometer consists of two legs, each containing a liquid of known specific gravity.

Mass Flowrate - The mass of fluid moving through a pipe or channel within a given period of time.

Master Black Belt - A teacher and mentor of black belts. Provides support, reviews projects, and undertakes larger scale projects.

Measured Variable - 1. The physical quantity, property, or condition which is to be measured. Common measured variables are temperatures, pressure, rate of flow, thickness, speed, etc. 2. The pan of the process that is monitored to determine the actual condition of the controlled variable.

Microprocessor - A large-scale integrated circuit that has all the functions of a computer, except memory and input/output systems. The IC thus includes the instruction set, ALU, registers and control functions.

Mixed Effects Model - Contains elements of both the fixed and random effects models.

Modularity - The degree to which a system of programs is developed in relatively independent components, some of which may be eliminated if a reduced version of the program is acceptable.

Multiloop Control - A control scheme that incorporates more than one feedback loop in order to ensure more precise control.

Nominal - Unordered categories which indicate membership or non-membership with no implication of quantity, i.e., assembly area number one, part numbers, etc.

Nonconforming Unit - A unit which does not conform to one or more specifications, standards, and/or requirements.

Nonvolatile Memory Output Module - Computer memory that retains data when power is removed.

Normal Distribution - A continuous, symmetrical density function characterized by a bell-shaped curve, e.g., distribution of sampling averages.

Null Hypothesis - A tentative explanation which indicates that a chance distribution is operating; a contrast to the null hypothesis.

Offset - A constant and steady state of deviation of the measured variable from the set point.

One-sided Alternative - The value of a parameter which has an upper bound or a lower bound, but not both.

Ordinal - Ordered categories (ranking) with no information about distance between each category, i.e., rank ordering of several measurements of an output parameter.

Ordinate - The vertical axis of a graph.

Orifice - A calibrated opening in a plate inserted in a fluid stream for measuring velocity of flow.

Output Module - This module may contain a digital-to-analog converter. Signals from this module go to the final control element which makes the required change to the process.

Parameter - A constant defining a particular property of the density function of a variable.

Pareto Diagram - A chart which ranks, or places in order, common occurrences.

Parity - The use of a self-checking code in a computer employing binary digits in which the total number of 1's or 0's in each permissible code expression is always even or always odd.

P Charts - Charts used to plot percent defectives in a sample.

Peripheral Device - Any device, distinct from the central processor, that can provide input to or accept output from the computer.

Perturbation - A non-random disturbance.

Potential Energy - Energy related to the position or height above a place to which fluid could possibly flow.

Power of an Experiment - The probability of rejecting the null hypothesis when it is false and accepting the alternate hypothesis when it is true.

Power Supply - The device within a computer that converts external AC power to internal DC voltage.

Precision - The degree of reproducibility among several independent measurements of the same true value.

Pressure Measurement - Any method of determining internal force per unit area in a process vessel, tank, or piping system due to fluid or compressed gas; this includes measurement of static or dynamic pressure, or absolute (total) or gage (total minus atmospheric) pressure, in any system of units.

Prevention - The practice of eliminating unwanted variation a priori (before the fact), e.g., predicting a future

Six Sigma Glossary

condition from a control chart and then applying corrective action before the predicted event transpires.

Primary Control Variable - The major independent variables used in the experiment.

Probability of an Event - The number of successful events divided by the total number of trials.

Process - A particular method of doing something, generally involving a number of steps or operations. A physical or chemical change of matter or conversion of energy, for example, a change in pressure, temperature, speed, electrical potential, et cetera.

Process Average - The central tendency of a given process characteristic across a given amount of time or at a specific point in time.

Process of Control Chart - Any of a number of various types of graphs upon which data are plotted against specific control limits.

Process Management - The cycle of continuous review, re-examination and renewal of fundamental work processes that contribute to an organization's performance and productivity. Itself a continual process, process management must at all times challenge a process' fit with other processes, and may result in radical change to work methods and practices.

Process Spread - The range of values which a given process characteristic displays; this particular term most often applies to the range but may also encompass the variance. The spread may be based on a set of data collected at a specific point in time or may reflect the variability across a given amount of time.

Producers Risk - Probability of rejecting a lot when, in fact, the lot should have been accepted (see ALPHA RISK).

Programmable Logic Controller (PLC) - A microprocessor-based industrial control system. It communicates with other process control components through data links. It is used in process control for simple switching tasks, PID control, complex data manipulation, arithmetic operations, timing and process and machine control.

Proportional Band - The change in input required to produce a full range change in output due to proportional control action. The preferred term is proportional gain.

Proportional Control - A control mode in which there is a continual linear relationship between the deviation computer in the controller, the signal of the controller, and the position of the final control element.

Proportional Gain - The ratio of change in output due to proportional control action to the change in input.

Proportional, Integral, Derivative Control (PID) - A combination of proportional, integral, and derivative control actions.

PSI - Abbreviation for pounds per square inch.

PSIA - Abbreviation for pounds per square inch, absolute.

PSIG - Abbreviation for pounds per square inch, gage.

R Charts - Plot of the difference between the highest and lowest in a sample. Range control chart.

Random Access Memory (RAM) - This is memory that can be written into or read from and allows access to any address within the memory. RAM is volatile in that contents are lost when the power is switched off.

Random Cause - A source of variation which is random; a change in the source ("trivial many" variables) will not produce a highly predictable change in the response (dependent variable), e.g., a correlation does not exist; any individual source of variation results in a small amount of variation in the response; cannot be economically eliminated from a process; an inherent natural source of variation.

Random Effects Model - Experimental treatments are a random sample from a larger population of treatments. Conclusions can be extended to the population. Interference's are not restricted to the experimental levels.

Randomness - A condition in which any individual event in a set of events has the same mathematical probability of occurrence as all other events within the specified set, i.e., individual events are not predictable even though they may collectively belong to a definable distribution.

Random Sample - One or more samples randomly selected from the universe (population).

Random Variable - A variable which can assume any value from a set of possible values.

Random Variations - Variations in data which result from causes which cannot be pinpointed or controlled.

Range - The difference between the highest and lowest values in a set of values or "subgroup."

Rankine - An absolute temperature scale in which the zero point is defined as absolute zero (the point where all spontaneous molecular activity ceases) and the scale divisions are equal to the scaled divisions in the Fahrenheit system; 0 F equals approximately 459.69.

Ranks - Values assigned to items in a sample to determine their relative occurrence in a population.

Ratio - Numeric scale which has an absolute zero point and equal units of measure throughout, i.e., measurements of an output parameter, i.e., amps.

Ratio Control - A control mode which is used to proportionally blend two of more raw materials.

Ratio Controller - A controller that maintains a predetermined ratio between two or more variables.

Read Only Memory (ROM) - Storage containing data that cannot be changed by computer instruction, but required alteration of construction circuits; therefore, data that is non-erasable and reusable, or fixed.

Reject Region - The region of values for which the alternate hypothesis is accepted.

Remote - In data processing, a term used to refer to any devices that are not located near the main computer.

Replication - Observations made under identical test conditions.

Robust - The condition or state in which a response parameter exhibits hermetically to external cause of a nonrandom nature; i.e., impervious to perturbing influence.

Representative Sample - A sample which accurately reflects a specific condition or set of conditions within the universe.

Resistance - The opposition to the flow of electricity in an electric circuit measured in ohms.

Resistance Temperature Detector - A component of a resistance thermometer that consists of a material whose electrical resistance is a known function of temperature.

Response Time - 1. The time required for the absolute value of the difference between the output and its final value to become and remain less than a specified amount, following the application of a step input or disturbance. 2. The time required for the output to first reach a definite value after the application of a step input or disturbance. 3. The time it takes for a controlled variable to react to a change in input.

RTD - A temperature transducer that provides temperature information as the change in resistance of a metal wire element, often platinum, as a function of temperature.

Sample - One or more observations drawn from a larger collection of observations or universe (population).

Scan Time- The time required for the CPU to read all inputs, execute the control program and update all local and remote I/Os.

Scatter Diagrams - Charts which allow the study of correlation, e.g., the relationship between two variables.

Self-Diagnostic Messages - Allow the controller to locate internal and some external faults.

Self-Tuning - A mode which continuously adjusts the tuning parameters as the process characteristics change.

Sensible Heat - Heat that causes a temperature change.

Sensor - A generic name for a device that detects either the absolute value of a physical quantity or a change in value of the quantity and converts the measurement into a useful input signal for an indicating or recording instrument.

Set Point - An input variable, which sets the desired value of the controlled variable. The input variable may be manually set, automatically set or programmed. It is expressed in the same units as the controlled variable.

Signal - The event or phenomenon that conveys data from one point to another.

Signal Conditioning - Processing the form or mode of a signal so as to make it intelligible to or compatible with any given device.

Single-Loop Control - In a process, one variable is controlled with either an analog or a digital controller.

Six Sigma - Sigma is a letter in the Greek alphabet. The term "sigma" is used to designate the distribution or spread about the mean (average) of any process or procedure.

For a business or manufacturing process, the sigma value is a metric that indicates how well that process is performing. The higher the sigma value, the better. Sigma measures the capability of the process to perform defect-free-work. A defect is anything that results in customer dissatisfaction.

Sigma is a statistical unit of measure which reflects process capability. The sigma scale of measure is perfectly correlated to such characteristics as defects-per-unit, parts-per million defective, and the probability of a failure/error. Meaning no more than 3.4 parts per Million.

Square Root Extractor - A component within the controller that receives a signal representing a non-linear process. The signal is linearized so that it can be correctly interpreted by the instrument.

Stable Process - A process which is free of assignable causes, e.g., in statistical control.

Standard Deviation - A statistical index of variability which describes the spread.

Statistical Control - A quantitative condition which describes a process that is free of assignable/special causes of variation, e.g., variation in the central tendency and variance. Such a condition is most often evidenced on a control chart, i.e., a control chart which displays an absence of nonrandom variation.

Six Sigma Glossary

Statistical Process Control - The application of statistical methods and procedures relative to a process and a given set of standards.

Subgroup - A logical grouping of objects or events which displays only random event-to-event variations, e.g., the objects or events are grouped to create homogenous groups free of assignable or special causes. By virtue of the minimum within group variability, any change in the central tendency or variance of the universe will be reflected in the "subgroup-to-subgroup' variability.

System - That which is connected according to a scheme.

System Memory - The memory which stores programs and data associated with the controller operation. System memory is often read-only memory.

Systematic Variables - A pattern which displays predictable tendencies.

Test of Significance - A procedure to determine whether a quantity subjected to random variation differs from a postulated value by an amount greater than that due to random variation alone.

Thermistor - A temperature transducer constructed from semiconductor material and for which temperature is converted into a resistance, usually with negative slope and highly nonlinear. Its usual applications are as a nonlinear circuit element (either alone or in combination with a heater), as a temperature compensator in a measurement circuit, or as a temperature measurement element.

Thermocouple - A temperature measuring instrument that develops voltage when heated based on the combined thermoelectric effect between two electrically connected conductors (usually wires) of dissimilar composition and the temperature difference between the connection (hot junction) and the other end of the conductors (cold junction).

Transducer - Any device or component that converts an input signal of one form to an output signal of another form-for instance, a piezoelectric transducer converts pressure waves into electrical signals, or vice versa.

Transmitter - A transducer which responds to a measured variable by means of a sensing element and converts it to a standardized transmission signal which is a function only of the measurement.

Tuning - The use of various techniques involving adjustments to both hardware and software to improve the operating efficiency of a computer system.

Two-Position Action - A type of control-system action that involves positioning the final control device in either of two fixed positions without permitting it to stop at any intermediate position.

Two-Sided Alternative - The values of a parameter which designate an upper and lower bound.

Unnatural Pattern - Any pattern in which a significant number of the measurements do not group them-selves around a center line; when the pattern is unnatural, it means that outside disturbances are present and are affecting the process.

Upper Control Limit - A horizontal line on a control chart (usually dotted) which represents the upper limits of process capability.

User Program - The program loaded into a PLC which contains the instructions to run the process or machine. The user program contains instructions that indicate what each output should be, based on the status of one or more specified inputs.

Variable - A characteristic that may take on different values.

Variables Data - Numerical measurements made at the interval or ratio level; quantitative data, e.g., ohms, voltage, diameter; subdivisions of the measurement scale are conceptually meaningful, e.g., 1.6478 volts.

Variation - Any quantifiable difference between individual measurements; such differences can be classified as being due to common causes (random) or special causes (assignable).

Voice of the Business – The stated mission, goals and business objectives of an organization. This collection of specific, documented statements of intent are the guidelines by which linkages are established between Six Sigma projects and targeted levels of improvement. The Voice of the Business should outline exactly what it is the business does, as well as how the business intents to accomplish its mission. Combined with the Voice of the Customer, the Voice of the Business plays an important role in defining potential Six Sigma projects.

Voice of the Customer – A systematic, institutionalized approach for eliciting and analyzing customers' requirements, expectations, level of satisfaction and areas of concern. Typically, a Voice of the Customer effort includes facilitated focus groups, individual interviews, surveys. The Voice of the Customer is a key data source in the Project Selection process.

Venturi Tube- A primary differential pressure producing device having a cone section approach to a throat and a longer cone discharge section. Used for high volume flow at low pressure loss.

Volatile Memory - Memory whose contents are lost when the power is switched off.

Volume - 1. The three-dimensional space occupied by an object. 2. A measure of capacity for a tank or other container in standard units.

Volumetric Flowrate - The volumes of fluid moving through a pipe or channel within a given period of time.

Vortex Shedding Flowmeter - A device that uses differential pressure variations associated with the forming and shedding of vortices in a stream of fluid flowing past a standard flow obstruction to actuate a sealed detector at a frequency that is proportional to vortex shedding, which, in turn, provides an output signal directly related to flow rate.

Wet Leg - The liquid-filled, low-side impulse line in a differential pressure measuring system.

Working Fluid - Fluid that does the work for a system.

X & R Charts - A control chart which is a representation of process capability over time; displays the variability in the process average and range across time.

Yellow Belt - A Yellow Belt is any employee who has received introductory training in the fundamentals of Six Sigma. The Yellow Belt gathers data, participates in problem-solving exercises and adds their personal experiences to the exploration process. Yellow Belts should have basic high school level math and reading skills.

Bibliography

Brusse, Warren. (2004) *Statistics for Six Sigma Made Easy!*. New York, New York. McGraw-Hill Companies Inc.

Sodhi, ManMohan, & Sodhi, Navdeep. (2008) *Six Sigma Pricing: Improving Pricing Operations To Increase Profits*. Upper Saddle River, New Jersey. FT Press.

George, Michael. (2003) *Lean Six Sigma For Service*. New York, New York. McGraw-Hill Companies Inc.

Pande, Pete, & Holpp, Larry. (2002) *What Is Six Sigma?*. New York, New York. McGraw-Hill Companies Inc.

Pyzdek, Thomas. (2003) *The Six Sigma Handbook: Revised and Expanded*. New York, New York. McGraw-Hill Companies Inc.

Cygi, Craig, & DeCarlo, Neil, & Williams, Bruce. (2005) *Six Sigma for Dummies*. Hoboken, New Jersey. Wiley Publishing Inc.

Keller, Paul. (2005) *Six Sigma Demystified: A Self-Teaching Guide*. New York, New York. McGraw-Hill Inc.

The Six Sigma Manual

Dedication & Author Biography

To Layla, for allowing me to follow a new path.

Craig Baird is a professional writer from British Columbia, who spends his time writing books and hiking the mountains around his home. Prior to being a writer he was a computer network administrator who was looking for a change. These days he spends his time writing books for himself, and his clients, from all over the world.

Baird's second book, *The Complete Guide to Investing in Index Funds – How to Earn High Rates of Return Safely*, will also be published by Atlantic Publishing Company in early 2009.

The Six Sigma Manual

Index

A

American Society for Quality, 107

ANOVA, 175, 8

Armand Feigenbaum, 21

B

Black Belt, 217-218, 100-109, 111-112, 114, 117, 122, 125, 259, 268, 6, 12

C

CDOV, 248, 252-253, 10

Champion, 95-96, 113, 260, 198

Charter, 70, 76-77, 199

Coach, 100, 104, 118

Control Factor, 54

Critical to Cost, 153-155, 7

Critical to Quality, 153-154, 156, 201-202, 204, 207-209, 213-214, 46, 50-51, 250-252, 4, 7

Critical to Schedule, 153, 156, 7

Critical to X, 46-47, 4

CTQ, 46, 50

CTX, 46-49

D

Data Storage, 181

DCCDI, 27, 248-249, 10

DCDOV, 27, 248, 250, 10

Defects per Million Opportunities, 37, 46, 59, 5

Define, 39, 54, 61, 79, 92-93, 114, 128-129, 131-132, 134-137, 144-146, 157, 177-179, 201-202, 204, 207-208, 196-198, 249-251

Design of Experiments, 35, 46, 52, 54, 100, 4

DFSS, 198, 12

DMADOV, 27, 248, 251, 10

DMADV, 201-205, 207, 211, 213, 217-220, 246, 27, 195-199, 248-249, 252, 255, 8

DMAIC, 148, 154, 156-157, 160-161, 175-177, 184, 186, 193-194, 201-202, 205, 207, 211, 213, 219, 246, 51, 70, 79, 117, 131-133, 135, 144-146, 21, 27, 127-128, 130, 196, 199, 222, 248-249, 252, 255, 6, 11

DOE, 46, 52, 54-55

E

Engineering Process Control, 187-188

Evaluation, 72-73, 119, 18, 6

Executive Leadership, 101

Experiment Error, 53-54

G

Gage Repeatability and Reproducibility, 55, 265

Green Belt, 100, 108-109, 111, 114, 118, 122, 265, 6

H

Hard Savings, 139-140

Hypothesis, 161, 64-67, 257, 259, 263, 269-270, 274

I

IDOV, 27, 248, 250, 10

Implementation, 214, 70, 79, 93, 96-98, 106, 265, 249, 6

Interaction, 53, 265, 267

Interactivity, 181

Internal Rate of Return, 183, 46, 56-57, 5

International Quality Federation, 107

Inventory, 163, 227, 229, 71, 140

K

Kaisen, 241

L

The Law of Complexity and Cost, 231

The Law of Flexibility, 230

The Law of Focus, 230

The Law of the Market, 230
The Law of Velocity, 231
Lean, 281, 225-226, 230-231, 233-236, 238-240, 245, 27, 221-223, 9-12
Level Loading, 168
Little's Law, 233, 238

M

Magnitude, 137-139, 142, 145, 258, 7
MAIC, 145, 27, 248-249, 10
Master Black Belt, 101-104, 106, 109, 111-112, 125, 268, 12
Mean, 150-152, 167, 171, 175, 190-191, 46, 79-80, 100, 131-132, 138, 260, 276, 14, 28, 128, 2, 7
Median, 150, 260, 7
Mentor, 100-101, 104, 119, 260, 268
Metrics, 153, 156, 202, 204-205, 217, 46, 57-58, 73, 93, 144, 262, 24, 129, 197, 251, 5, 7
Mode, 149-150, 260, 272, 274-276, 7
Modeling, 69, 80-81, 27, 5
Motorola, 34-38, 44, 82, 100-101, 107, 13, 19, 23, 12

N

Negotiation, 119
Net Present Value, 183, 56
Non-value Activities, 166, 168,
Number of Processes, 181

O

One-way Analysis, 175
Operational Procedure, 189
Optimization, 179, 24
Overproduction, 225-227, 231, 245, 9

P

Potential Savings, 140
Primary Variable, 53
Problem Statement, 137, 140-142, 145, 7
Process Cycle Efficiency, 234, 238
Project Objective, 142, 7

Q

Quality Function Deployment, 162

R

Randomization, 181, 53-54

Range, 151, 91, 271-273, 280, 7, 11

Refresher, 121

Reinforcement, 119-120, 6

Replication, 54, 274

Response Variable, 53, 262

S

Scientific Method, 62-67, 82, 5

Simulation, 180-181, 184, 215-216, 218

SIPOC, 46, 59, 61, 5

Six Sigma Glossary, 257, 10

The Six Sigma Manual, 2, 11

Soft Savings, 139-140

Special Causes of Variation, 276

Standard Deviation, 276, 16

Statistical Process Control, 187, 260, 277

Statistics, 281, 35-36, 148-149, 151-152, 157, 181, 207, 82, 108, 146, 16, 25, 7

T

Total Quality Management, 20-21, 2, 4

Type 1 Waste, 162

Type 2 Waste, 162, 166

V

Value Stream Analysis, 162, 8

Variation, 34, 151, 170-175, 181, 188, 46, 51, 53, 55, 258, 263-265, 270, 272-273, 276-277, 279, 14, 16

Y

Yellow Belt, 112, 280